Plaited Basketry
with Birch Bark

Vladimir Yarish, Flo Hoppe & Jim Widess

STERLING

New York / London
www.sterlingpublishing.com

Text by Vladimir Yarish, Flo Hoppe, and Jim Widess
"Notes from Novgorod" historical chapters 1–5 by Vladimir Yarish
Photos in chapters 1–5 by Vladimir Yarish, unless otherwise noted.
All other photos in book by Jim Widess, unless otherwise noted.
Baskets created by Vladimir Yarish unless otherwise noted or replicated
based on museum artifacts and those found in archeological excavations.

We're grateful to the Novgorod State Museum of History, Architecture,
and Fine Arts for allowing study and photos of birch-bark artifacts
shown in this book.

STERLING and the distinctive Sterling logo are
registered trademarks of Sterling Publishing Co., Inc.

Library of Congress Cataloging-in-Publication Data

Yarish, Vladimir.
  Plaited basketry with birch bark / Vladimir Yarish, Flo Hoppe & Jim
Widess.
      p. cm.
  Includes bibliographical references and index.
  ISBN 978-1-4027-4809-7
  1. Basketwork. 2. Birch bark. I. Hoppe, Flo, 1942- II. Widess, Jim.
III. Title.
  TT879.B3Y37 2008
  746.41'2--dc22

                                        2008008864

10 9 8 7 6 5 4 3 2 1

Published by Sterling Publishing Co., Inc.
387 Park Avenue South, New York, NY 10016
© 2009 by Vladimir Yarish, Flo Hoppe, and Jim Widess
Illustrations on page 48 © 2008 by Kevin Downs
Distributed in Canada by Sterling Publishing
℅ Canadian Manda Group, 165 Dufferin Street
Toronto, Ontario, Canada M6K 3H6
Distributed in the United Kingdom by GMC Distribution Services
Castle Place, 166 High Street, Lewes, East Sussex, England BN7 1XU
Distributed in Australia by Capricorn Link (Australia) Pty. Ltd.
P.O. Box 704, Windsor, NSW 2756, Australia

Printed in China
All rights reserved

Book design and layout by *tabula rasa* graphic design

Sterling ISBN 978-1-4027-4809-7

For information about custom editions, special sales, premium
and corporate purchases, please contact Sterling Special Sales
Department at 800-805-5489 or specialsales@sterlingpublishing.com.

In blessed memory of my parents, Lidiya Alekseyevna Yarish and Ivan Isayevich Yarish
—Vladimir Yarish

To my husband, Don, who shared in the birch bark harvesting
in the dangerous Russian forest
—Flo Hoppe

To my wife and partner in life, Sher, and our son, Andy,
who give me so much encouragement and love
—Jim Widess

Contents

Foreword

This book wouldn't be complete without mentioning how it all began—Vladimir's introduction to basketry, how he first came to the United States, and how we began working together. Little did we know back in 1994 that we would continue to collaborate 13 years later.

In 1984, a friend gave Vladimir a small piece of birch bark for his birthday. Since he had always enjoyed making things by hand, he asked his friend to show him how to make a few baskets. His friend showed him how to make three; after that, Vladimir was on his own. As he learned and gained experience in weaving, he began to study the uses and centuries-old history of birch bark. His musical study and career gave way to full-time basketry, and in 1993 he became a birch-craft teacher with an active studio and many students at the Cultural Palace in Velikiy Novgorod.

In 1994 he was asked to go to the United States to take part in the International Children's Festival at Wolf Trap Farm Park in Vienna, Virginia. The first time he was asked, he was reluctant and refused to go. However, in time he was persuaded that it was an excellent opportunity and he should travel to the States. He was assigned to teach children how to make a small birch-bark bead during the festival and to give talks to interested groups. Because thousands of children would be attending, the High Country Basketry Guild was asked to aid in teaching. A number of guild members,

including me, volunteered to help. Although the small bead was a challenge, the kids went away pleased. With an interpreter's help, Vladimir also gave a talk and demonstration to our guild. Three lucky weavers got to try their hands at it and went home with a basket.

The next year, Vladimir invited a group of Americans to take part in the cultural celebration in his city. Performing dance groups and artisans came from all over Russia and other parts of the world. Our invitation was accepted, the paperwork done, and a quilter, a photographer, and a basket maker (me) as well as a dance troupe went to Russia. I also had reservations about the trip and said "no" the first time asked. But fortunately, I was persuaded to go. I taught children how to make Native American dream catchers at the fair and at several schools; the dream catcher was and continues to be extremely popular. And we met wonderful, generous, warm people everywhere we went.

Later, at the Association of Michigan Basketmakers (AMB), I was struck with the idea to have Vladimir teach at a convention. I was taking a class from Kathy Tessler and discussed the possibility with her. With her encouragement, I wrote a letter to Vladimir and suggested a possible schedule. He taught at AMB in 1997 and has been back to America frequently ever since. We have progressed from letters to e-mails and from visits of a few weeks to a few months, and Vladimir has gained fluency in English, and, with a little push from American weavers, an appreciation of contemporary basketry.

I believe the best form of diplomacy occurs when people get together to talk, work, and live. Vladimir and I have been lucky to meet and stay with so many Americans here. And I have been extremely fortunate to have met and visited so many Russians, thanks to Vladimir and his wife Tatiana. Since travel to Russia is easier now, numerous American basket makers have been able to visit Vladimir at his studio or home.

Comparing Basket Weaving in Russia and North America

Basket makers everywhere learn the basic weaving technique of over one, under one. While the process may differ in our two countries, the results are much the same.

In the United States and Canada, mostly women take informal weaving classes, often in adult-education or community centers, for enjoyment. We usually start with classes using flat or round reeds, learning a little about the many different North American styles found in a broad-brush approach. The teacher usually prepares the materials and buys supplies for the students.

In Russia, students take classes at local cultural centers, such as that where Vladimir teaches, for the enjoyment of weaving. Students, however, focus on the traditional style and one material, birch bark. They trek into mosquito-infested forests to harvest their own bark for weaving; it is not the teacher's job to prepare materials. Classes are held once a week for nine months (September to May), during which students learn to develop basketry skills using birch bark, beginning with the most basic and progressing to more complex baskets.

Students devote a long time to their weaving; some of Vladimir's students have been working with him for 10 to 12 years.

Our native teaching styles also differ. American teachers might tell a student: "It could be better if you fix it." But Vladimir is more direct: "It's no good—take the strip out."

In the United States, week-long weaving sessions at art schools and basketry conventions have become great learning experiences. Students by the hundreds come for classes in new techniques, learn from several teachers, and use a variety of basket materials. The three- to four-day conventions also allow weaving students to share experiences with one another. These conventions also serve as a social experience.

In Russia, such gatherings from near and far to learn basket weaving just don't happen—except in Vladimir's studio. Men and women come from long distances to take concentrated week-long courses. Most are advanced weavers who sell their baskets, and they want to learn more to sell more and better baskets.

In North America, some of us remain generalists, and some specialize in a particular style or material. In Russia, people stick with materials they can harvest—birch bark—and hone their skills, taking a more serious approach.

We all like to create baskets, because we enjoy creating something with our own hands, and some of us eventually sell our work. Universally, weavers enjoy the social aspects of weaving together, not to mention the classes, chai tea, delicious food, and conversations that follow.

—Ann Harrow

Ann Harrow introduced Vladimir Yarish to American and Canadian basketry and encouraged him to teach in the States and for exchange visits in his Novgorod studio.

Introduction *by Jim Widess*

Just as bamboo is the most important tree in Japan, cedar in the Pacific Northwest, coconut palm in Polynesia, and rattan in Southeast Asia, for centuries, birch has remained the most important tree for the peoples of the deciduous forests in northern Europe, Scandinavia, North America, Siberia, and those who live in the subpolar regions of Europe and Asia.

The birch tree, with its white bark and young, deep reddish-brown branches, thrives in almost any soil or climate. The wood is soft and used for barrel staves and broom handles. Its twigs are utilized for wattlework in walls and thatching for roofs. The roots are used for stitching baskets and other containers. Its bark is used for shelters, containers, boat shells, paper, glue, and medical antiseptics, and its sap for a sweetener and beer. The specific fungus that grows on the tree is used as a fire starter and as felt for clothing. Birch bark has a natural resistance to fungus. It has been employed to treat sore throats, frostbite, abrasions, and cuts to the skin. Organic substances can be preserved in birch-bark containers. In addition, chewing birch bark helps maintain dental health, because birch bark contains xylitol, a substance that suppresses the growth of the harmful bacteria that cause cavities.

In 1991 a preserved body was found trapped in a glacier in the Ötztal Alps on the Italian-Swiss border. Some of the belongings found with this 5,500-year-old Neolithic traveler (known as "Ötzi the Iceman") can give us a vivid picture of the importance of the birch tree to these early inhabitants. His copper axe head was attached to the axe handle with a tar made from birch bark, and his flint arrowheads and feathers were attached to the arrow shafts with this tar, as well. He carried two birch-bark containers stitched with fiber from the inner bark of the linden tree. In one of the containers, he probably carried pieces of glowing charcoal embers from the previous night's campfire, which, wrapped in fresh maple leaves for insulation, would still be smoldering when he needed to start another fire that evening. A birch fungus that he carried on his wrist had antiseptic healing qualities were he injured. Another birch fungus he used as tinder to catch the spark he made by striking his flint knife on a small chunk of pyrite if his embers went out. It is likely that when he reached a lower altitude, he would use lengths of freshly harvested birch bark for insulation as a ground cover. If he were to stay in one area for any length of time, then he might build a structure out of birch saplings and cover it with sheets of birch bark for a more permanent shelter.

At the end of the last Ice Age, as the climate began to warm and the glaciers started to melt, the newly exposed land became very wet and the people of the area had to decide whether to move north into the ice regions and follow the reindeer or move south into the drier regions where agriculture would be a challenge. Later, as the wet, boggy regions began to dry, the birch trees moved into these meadows and became the climax forest in the subpolar regions. As the reindeer migrated north and then south, the birch-tree forests became the wintering grounds and the sub-Arctic residents learned to use the tree for many aspects of their life, utilizing the bark for shelters, waterproof containers, adhesives, and medicines.

Analyzing archeological sites, we find that the use of birch bark goes back at least 10,000 years. Birch tar is a brownish-black product obtained by heating birch bark with a limited supply of air. Mesolithic and Neolithic finds of shapeless masses with tooth impressions have been discovered in several prehistoric sites in Scandinavia, southern Germany, and Switzerland, indicating that birch tar was chewed to make an adhesive.

The making of fire was critical to the survival of these Stone Age inhabitants. Even wet birch bark will ignite for a fire after simply being wiped dry. And the touchwood fungus that grows naturally on birch trees is thought to be the best source of tinder, the material for catching a spark made by flint and marcassite. The fungus *(Fomes fomentarius)* is cut into thin slices, washed in a weak alkali, and then beaten with a rock or hammer to make it into a soft, feltlike cloth that could be easily torn into pieces. The felt was then charred and afterward soaked in strong urine. The touchwood felt could be kept smoldering with very little heat so that fire could be transported over long distances. This Neolithic technology remained virtually unchanged until the invention of matches.

Items made from plaited bark have been found in archeological sites in Finland. It is thought that the technique of plaiting was brought to Sweden by Finnish colonization beginning in the Middle Ages.

Large numbers of Arabic silver coins dating from the seventh century to the eleventh century found in Scandinavian and northwest Russian archeological sites testify to the extensive trade routes that Islamic merchants had established. Northern people were known to Muslim geographers as the "nomads of the sea."

Some treasures of the North were furs, especially sable, mink, ermine, fox, and otter. While furs were in demand in the higher altitudes of Central Asia, they were also used to trim the fashionable garments of the wealthy merchants of Central Asia and were as highly prized as the Chinese silks that the Islamic merchants also traded. The Turks prized amber from the shores of the Baltic as amulets. Walrus and narwhal ivory became dagger handles in Egypt. Honey and beeswax from northeastern Europe were highly sought after by the early Muslims. Birch bark was another valuable commodity as a source of paper for documents. Their purchases were also in exchange for Islamic silver coins, which became the currency of preference in the northern regions of Europe and Asia. At the same time, Scandinavian traders were colonizing the North Atlantic as well as traveling southeast to establish new trade centers in Kiev and Novgorod.

—Jim Widess

Note: Please refer to the metric equivalents chart on page 273 for metric and U.S. conversions.

Sewn birch-bark dish, made by Jim Widess.

Athabascan birch-bark tray, made with Alaska birch bark, split willow, and willow shoot for the rim, 14 × 10 × 3 inches. Collection of Ed and Katherine Rossbach.

Athabascan birch-bark box, made with willow bark, leather, a glass bead, and string, 9 × 9 × 5 inches. Collection of Ed and Katherine Rossbach.

Part I

Birch-Bark Craft History & Techniques

Notes from Novgorod

My obsession with birch bark began, quite innocently, in 1984 when a friend presented me with a small birch-bark piece for my birthday. I didn't then imagine that this seemingly insignificant event would alter my life so completely.

After plaiting my first three baskets, I was on my own. Since then, I have continued to weave and to study the uses and history of birch bark, a history that dates back centuries. My studies of music and the accordion gave way to the creation of baskets. In 1993 I became a teacher; my active studio has many long-term students at the Cultural Palace in the city of Velikiy Novgorod, Russia. I have published numerous articles about birch-bark basketry, its history, and the uses of special canisters. I have also organized or participated in exhibitions of birch-bark crafts in Velikiy Novgorod, Moscow, St. Petersburg, and many other Russian cities.

Today, I've dedicated myself to transferring the knowledge of this craft to as many people as possible. I teach adults birch-bark plaiting along with other traditional crafts through-out the week in my studio. Birch bark and its medieval history in Novgorod Oblast (province) has encouraged me to write a doctoral thesis on the topic. Fortunately, Novgorod boasts excellent museum collections of the birch-bark crafts still in remarkably good shape. This allows vital research and has deepened my love affair with birch bark.

As a birch-bark basketry artisan and teacher, I made my first trip to the United States in 1994 to participate in the International Children's Festival in Washington, D.C. Since then, I have taught at Association of Michigan Basketmakers and North Carolina Basketmakers' Association conventions, Midwest Basketry Focus, and other gatherings throughout the United States. I have also taught birch-bark basketry in France, Germany, Norway, and Taiwan.

I was born in Kazakhstan in 1954 but moved to Velikiy Novgorod in 1980, where I live with my wife Tatiana and our son George.

In chapters 1 to 5, I share some of my insights and learning about this traditional craft as it was practiced in Novgorod from medieval times.

—Vladimir Yarish

chapter one

Centuries of a Living Craft

Over the centuries, birch-bark creative arts and crafts developed and thrived in such far-flung parts of the world as China, Russia, Belarus, Latvia, Estonia, Finland, Sweden, Norway, and North America (the United States and Canada).

Birch bark has many qualities that account for the steadfast attention it drew from ancient artisans. It has long been known that birch bark both resists moisture and possesses antiseptic qualities. Birch-bark cells contain a fatty waxy acid, suberin. This substance makes the bark flexible, waterproof, and resistant to moderate acids and oils. Suberin does not dissolve in water or alcohol. Birch contains a high percentage of another substance, betulinol, making it antiseptic and resistant to microorganisms. The latter quality makes it extremely useful for storing food and other perishable products. However, when contemporary artists use glue or plywood in the creation of an object from birch bark, they destroy the natural qualities of the material.

Birch bark adapts well to ornamentation through a variety of techniques. It can be decorated with paints, slit with a knife, pressed with stamps, or drawn on with an awl. Because birch bark is many-layered, a sharp tool can be used to scrape away the

Northwest Russia consists of several regions, including Novgorod Oblast (or province). (Oblast means an administrative territorial division within the Russian Federation as well as other former Soviet republics, or simply, "province.") One of the main cities in Novgorod province is the medieval city of Novgorod-the-Great, also known today as Velikiy Novgorod. (*Velikiy* means "the Great" and *Novgorod* means "new city.") This city dates from the ninth century, when it was the capital of the Novgorodian Republic. For more about this medieval city, see chapter 2.

bark, cutting and taking out the top layer or two. One unusual way of decorating the bark is by biting a pattern into it with the teeth, a technique found in North America (notably by the Ojibwa who call this centuries-old folk art *mazinibaganjigan*), Siberia, and medieval Novgorod.

Artisans have used birch bark in basically two ways. Native North Americans used birch bark in sheets, sewing it with roots of cedar or American pine. Russians, Finns, and Scandinavians, on the other hand, primarily made their products by weaving.

The work of Siberian peoples is very similar to that of the people in northern China. The Siberian and Chinese peoples, as well as the native tribes of North America, made their products only from sheets of birch bark, often bending the whole sheets and then sewing with various materials (a root, sinews of animals, horse hair, and so forth). Or they made designs with several sheets of birch bark. The peoples of Belarus, the Baltic States (Latvia, Estonia, Lithuania), Scandinavia (Danes, Swedes, and Norwegians but rarely Icelanders), Finland, and Russia usually engaged in weaving.

Therefore, the Native North Americans share commonalities with Siberians, the Siberian work resembles the Chinese, and Russians have elements in common with other so-called birch-bark nationalities. In Norway, artisans produced canisters, boxes,

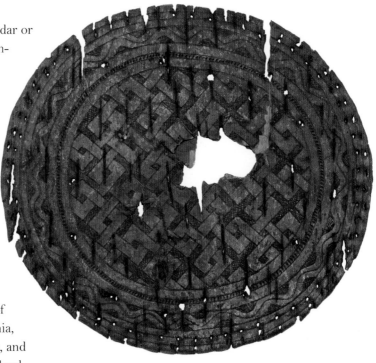

Lid of *tues* ("vessel used mainly for liquids"), with compass ornaments, dating from the first part of the thirteenth century, diameter 5 1/2 inches. Photo by Evgeniy Gordyushenkov.

Biting on lid recreated by Vladimir Yarish.

and bags from birch-bark sheets until the early sixteenth century, when Finnish immigrants introduced weaving.

Finns are not Scandinavians, but they are often casually grouped today with the neighboring Scandinavians. The Finns' origins differ, and Finnish belongs to the Finno-Ugrian language group, which resembles no Scandinavian languages.

In the seventh century, Slavic tribes from along the Dnieper River traveled north to the European part of present-day Russia, where Finnish tribes lived. It is possible to assume that the ancient Slavs as well as ancient Swedes and Norwegians adopted the technique of weaving birch bark from the numerous

Lid of tues, with biting design, thirteenth century, diameter 3 1/2 inches. Photo by Evgeniy Gordyushenkov.

Lid of tues, with compass ornaments, dating from the second part of the fourteenth century through the beginning of the fifteenth century, diameter 5 inches. Photo by Evgeniy Gordyushenkov.

Finnish tribes who at one time were spread from Scandinavia to the Ural Mountains and beyond.

In Russia, there are a few places where archeologists are able to extract medieval wooden objects. One of them is Novgorod-the-Great, a city founded in A.D. 859. Due to the special quality of the soil there, the organic materials thrown out or lost by people many centuries ago can be preserved. From the wooden artifacts extracted, we have been able to learn about the city's position as one of the largest European cultural centers by the fourteenth century with a developed network of arts and crafts in which birch-bark crafts flourished.

Birch is truly a universal tree. It is difficult to find any area of country life in northwest Russia where the birch, both as a tree and as other materials derived from it, was not in use. It was used for firewood and for the preparation of tar (as a special lubricant), its branches were used in the Russian bath, and the shepherd's musical instruments were made from it. Various household utensils were made from birch, as were containers for moving heavy objects, footwear, every conceivable kind of purse and bag, and many other items.

The birch tree has long held a special place in Russian folk culture, and plays a role in many national ceremonies and customs. The birch influenced the lives of Native North Americans from the cradle to the grave.

Note: Some transliterations of Russian words are given here; for more transliterations of Russian words or for more detailed transliterations, refer to the glossary on pp. 271–272.

Lid of tues (three layers—the upper layer is woven), thirteenth century, diameter 8 inches. Photo by Evgeniy Gordyushenkov.

Body of tues, with woven exterior and view of inside seam, thirteenth century, height 2¼ inches, diameter 3¼ inches. Photo by Evgeniy Gordyushenkov.

According to eyewitnesses, when the first immigrants from Europe to northeast America arrived at the beginning of the seventeenth century, they found the native people engaged in the seasonal hunt for birch bark. The birch also played an important role in peasant life in northern China, where it was used widely in the household.

It is known that people in medieval Novgorod wore leather footwear and that *lapti* ("shoes woven from birch bark") appeared much later. The first birch-bark shoe was found only in the archeological layers of the fifteenth century and cannot be dated before then.

Archeologists assume that lapti became widely used in Russia in the sixteenth century although they existed for several earlier centuries and were worn by workers in rural communities. In Novgorod during the medieval period, not only were birch-bark articles produced from birch-bark sheets, but they were woven as well. This is proven by the presence in the Novgorod State Museum of History, Architecture, and Fine Arts (it has many branches and is sometimes also called the Novgorod State United Museum or more simply, the Novgorod museum) of many prepared birch-bark strips and two *kostyki* ("special tools of the weaver") dating from the thirteenth and fifteenth centuries. The overwhelming majority of exhibits in the Novgorod archeological collection are fragments of products made from birch-bark sheets—*tuesi* ("special vessels made primarily for liquids"), *lukoshki* ("baskets without handles"), and various boxes. But due to the woven fragments also on display, it can be assumed that they wove lapti, bags, and articles resembling backpacks. Many examples of fishing tackle (floats and sinkers) made

Fragment of painted bark ornamented with braiding and lines, dating from the second part of the thirteenth century, 8½ × 3 inches.

Strip with biting design, dating from the end of the eleventh century, 11 × 2 inches.

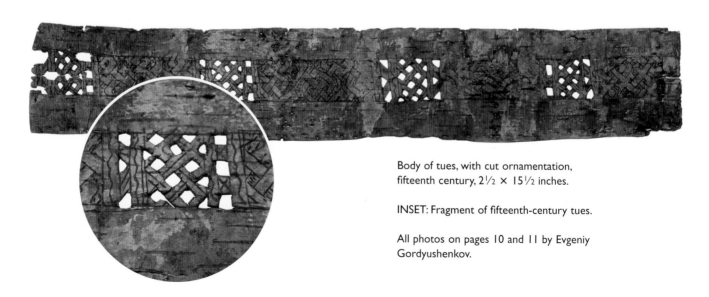

Body of tues, with cut ornamentation, fifteenth century, 2½ × 15½ inches.

INSET: Fragment of fifteenth-century tues.

All photos on pages 10 and 11 by Evgeniy Gordyushenkov.

Lid of box, middle of the thirteenth century,
7¼ × 12 inches.

INSET: Fragment of thirteenth-century lid.

using birch-bark strips have been found in archeological excavations. In addition, birch-bark items whose use so far cannot be explained by researchers have been excavated.

The most important Novgorod artifacts found during archeological excavations are the birch-bark scrolls, which are letters written on birch bark. The 959th such letter was found in 2006 in an excavation on the territory of the city. Considering that archeologists estimate that less than 3 percent of the city is under excavation, it is possible to conclude that the Novgorodians of the Middle Ages were well-educated people who wrote letters to each other often and on all vital subjects.

It is hard to tell when the clever techniques once used for stitching together parts of birch-bark articles in medieval Novgorod

disappeared. The majority of such articles were sewn with cordage made from the bast (the internal part of the bark) of the linden tree. They probably disappeared during the period when *skoloten* ("birch-bark cylinders pulled from the tree in one piece") were "invented" or brought to the Novgorod lands, and artisans began to justify the use of a wooden bottom that was hammered into the well-steamed bottom part of an article, instead of using a birch-bark bottom.

The Yakuts and other peoples of Siberia attached bottoms to their containers, but they did it in a different manner than was practiced in medieval Novgorod. The seams securing them that had been preferred in medieval Novgorod became a lost art. Birch-bark crafts have changed gradually through

Scroll 363, "The Nerevskiy Excavation" (the name of the place where the scroll was found), dating from the last 20 years of the fourteenth century. Photo by Evgeniy Gordyushenkov.

This is the text of the scroll: "A bow from Semyon to my bride. If, perhaps, you don't remember, then keep in mind that you had some malt. There is rye malt in the storeroom. Take a cupful, as much flour as you need, and bake an ample pie. There is meat in cold storage. As for giving Ignat a ruble, give it to him."

The text of the scroll in Russian: Перевод (translation from old Russian into contemporary Russian): «Поклон от Семена невестке моей. Если, может быть, ты не помнишь, то имей в виду: у тебя солод был. Солод ржаной в подклете. Ты возьми пригоршню, а муки сколько нужно, и испеки пирога в меру. А мясо на сеннике. А что касается того, чтобы дать рубль Игнату, то ты дай».

the centuries. In the rural countryside, birch-bark designs became simpler, and technically complex elements began to disappear. Methods of fastening also changed and became simpler. Therefore, after the fifteenth century, more woven products have been exhibited in Novgorod. Although complicated to make, the stitched designs from birch-bark sheets with the intricate ornamentation of the people of Novgorod in the Middle Ages did not correspond to the aesthetic tastes of simple country life. Products necessary for daily use had to be strong and to be produced quickly.

For the last two centuries, Novgorod peasants have basically woven on the diagonal. In the ethnographic collections of the Novgorod State Museum of History, Architecture, and Fine Arts, plain-weaving products represent a small percentage of woven items. Tuesi were rarely produced in that same period. While the museum exhibits hundreds of woven products, it has only a few dozen tuesi. However, tuesi have been made in some locations in the Ural Mountains and in northwest Russia.

In the Novgorod villages today, few villagers can weave *stupni* and *bereshcheniki*. The footwear, which resembles galoshes, is meant to be worn in a courtyard, not for long distances. These shoes were typically left at the threshold, and women put them on to go milk the cow, for example. At other times they were worn to mow grass or pick berries in the woods. Stupni were primarily female footwear and were woven both symmetrically as well as asymmetrically, that is, for the left and right foot. They were woven from the toe, and the upper part can be woven in four different ways.

Birch-bark lapti were less common than lapti made entirely with linden-tree bark, but the part of birch-bark lapti that serves as tabs or eyelets (apertures or holes) for threading or attaching the laces is typically made completely of linden bark. For birch-bark lapti, weaving begins at the heel, not the toe. (The Russian word *lapti* is plural; *lapot* is the singular term.) Birch-bark stupni, in contrast, are worn without special tabs to attach them to feet, so that they can be used as galoshes.

Birch-bark boots were woven even more rarely. After World War II, because footwear

Asymmetrical stupni, typically used as galoshes, made in Novgorod province in late 20th century.

Asymmetrical stupni made by Vladimir Yarish, replicating the style made in the late 20th century.

Birch-bark lapot (singular of *lapti*) with linden bark, made in the late 20th century. Around the heel and ankle at the top of the lapot are four eyelets (apertures or holes) for threading lace to secure the shoe.

Linden-bark lapti with leather ropes, or laces, from Novgorod province, 1970s.

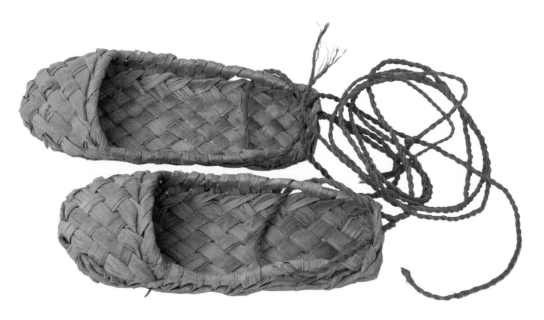

Linden-bark lapti with linden, inner-bark (bast) ropes, or laces, from Novgorod province, late 20th century.

was not to be found in the shops, Novgorod peasants in the Moshenskoe district made birch-bark boots for children. Several pairs of birch-bark boots are exhibited in the Novgorod State Museum of History, Architecture, and Fine Arts. Also in the museum are small booties woven for a child. These booties were probably woven at one time for a large rag doll as well.

Twenty-five years ago, art historians at the Novgorod museum considered birch-bark weaving a forgotten craft that existed in their province until the 1950s with no hope of revival. They did not think there was a reason to practice or develop the craft, even

Plain-woven lapti, made in a style more typical of those found in Finland or south Russia and unlike those made in the Novgorod area; late 20th century. Purchased in a shop.

Linden-bark lapot (single lapti), shown worn on the foot with a long lace attached to the shoe that extends up the calf.

for souvenirs. In that stagnant time before Perestroika, that seemed to be a valid argument. Novgorod museum staff noted that they found only three masters in Novgorod villages working with birch bark. Birch-bark weaving and other crafts were not actively practiced or developed in the late twentieth century, although they had not entirely disappeared. From time to time, new local artisans have appeared in the province. While there are few of them, there are enough so that rural crafts have not died away completely.

In the last decade, we managed to find six artisans working with birch bark in the Novgorod region. Not one of them was a professional craftsman, and each has tried many trades and developed specialties. All were trained in childhood by their grandfathers or

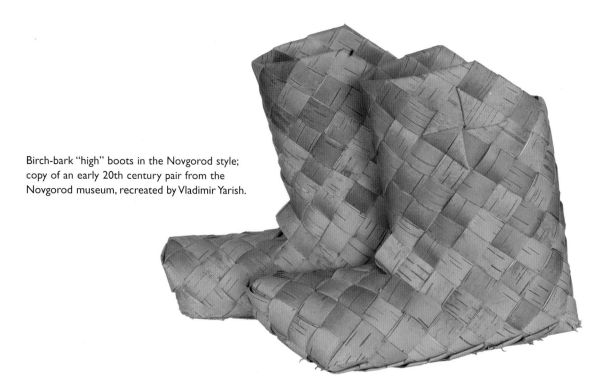

Birch-bark "high" boots in the Novgorod style; copy of an early 20th century pair from the Novgorod museum, recreated by Vladimir Yarish.

other relatives. Throughout their lives, they were not engaged in weaving on a regular basis. Their means of preparation, storage, and the way they work with birch bark, and the types of hand-made products, represent the mainstream of birch-bark craftsmanship as it developed in northwest Russia.

Traditional crafts, including making birch-bark baskets, are actively being made today in modern Russia. Some are produced as souvenirs while other works are more serious and based on tradition. We have begun to see a revival of the great culture of artistic handicrafts in Russia.

chapter two

Medieval Novgorod's Birch-Bark Crafts

Novgorodian birch-bark artifacts from the Middle Ages hold a special place among birch-bark crafts. Nowhere else did archeologists discover such a large number of birch-bark artifacts dating from the tenth to fifteenth centuries as in Novgorod. Since 1932, more than a thousand fragments of birch-bark household utensils alone have been found in excavations and stored in the Novgorod State Museum of History, Architecture, and Fine Arts and its branches, which include collections of archeology, architecture, fine arts, sciences, history, and more.

The first settlements of Slavs on the shores of Lake Ilmen have been traced to the end of the seventh century. It took about two centuries for a city to develop there. The first written source places Novgorod in the year A.D. 859, considered the founding date of the city.

By the fourteenth century, Novgorod was one of the largest cities in Europe. As trade in Novgorod flourished, it was comparable to major international trading centers like Amsterdam.

The city's history has been full of highs and lows. In trying to subject Novgorod to Moscow, tsars Ivan III and Ivan IV (better known as Ivan the Terrible) razed the city to its foundations. It was annexed to Moscow in 1478.

Novgorod remained the largest trade and crafts center until the beginning of the eighteenth century, when Peter the Great decided to build a new capital of the Russian state, St. Petersburg, on the banks of the River Neva. All transportation then streamed through St. Petersburg to Europe, and Novgorod lost its influence and became a small provincial town. Active building ceased, which proved to be a positive event for future archeologists since that meant that the soil was less disturbed within the city's limits.

In 1778, a new town plan with regular construction was approved. In contrast with the more spontaneous building of the past,

A "hen" rattle, a shape from the early nineteenth century, from Arkhangelsk Province, 4 × 2 × 3 inches. Recreated by Vladimir Yarish.

Round box, 12 × 7¼ inches made by Vladimir Yarish, 2002. Its construction is based on study of archeological remnants. The box's inside and bottom are shown in the two photos below.

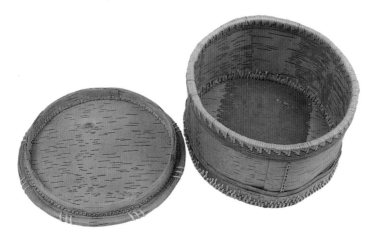

Inside of the lid and round box.

Lid and bottom of the round box.

streets flowed away from the centers of intensive life in the old city, which helped preserve its culture.

It is precisely due to this historical development that the centuries-old cultural layers were untouched by the stone structures built in other major Russian cities. Novgorod soil preserved all the multifaceted objects used in the daily life of the people, which experts have been able to study since 1932, when the city began systematic archeological excavations.

The city's soil has meant that the huge evidence of various human activities in earlier centuries has been preserved for archeologists. Increased water content in the clay favored the preservation of organic matter such as wood, leather, bones, remnants of food, and clothing. Metal objects were covered with a thin layer of corrosion but were not destroyed completely. The water-soaked soil with its relative absence of free oxygen also protected such articles from exposure to oxygen and air, which would have hastened decomposition. The primary building and ornamental material in medieval Novgorod was wood.

Because of the abundant precipitation in these wetlands, the city's residents did not dig wells or cellars or build deep foundations for their wooden homes. In other words, they did not carry out the kind of work that would disturb the city's soil.

Streets in medieval Novgorod were paved with wooden logs because the soil there and in the surrounding wetlands was swampy and the high humidity and rainfall created still more puddles and mud. As the logs eventually sank in the marshy soil, rotted, or were no longer fit for use, new logs were simply laid on top of them. On the average, this occurred every 17 to 20 years. During the 500 years from the tenth to the fifteenth century, these roadways were replaced about 30 times. The layer archeologists study in various places in the city today reaches about 22 to 26 feet. People in the past strolling on these roadways threw litter from their pockets, and people in their wooden homes discarded their trash in a corner of the manor courtyard. Wooden homes burned down, but their foundations, the bottom logs, were preserved in the marshy soil.

The most prolific cultural layers in Novgorod are from the tenth to the fifteenth century. The later cultural strata are not as rich. Beginning in the sixteenth century, the city lost its exceptional significance in the history of the state, and life gradually took on the characteristics of provincialism. The population decreased. Another reason is that the ground was always wet, except during the frozen winter and hot summer days. This bothered the residents, who finally in the late 1500s through the 1600s constructed a wooden drainage system, allowing water to flow from the city into the Volkhov River. The new drainage system began to actively destroy the later strata of earth that might have revealed significant cultural layers.

Today, the collection of excavated objects is truly uncountable and includes thousands and thousands of articles, from ancient coins and birch-bark scrolls (letters written on birch bark) to fragments of boats and ships.

Archeologists estimate that they have studied less than 3 percent of the available cultural layer under examination. The excavated areas are principally where new buildings were planned to be constructed. For the most part, artifacts have been dated by dendrochronology (tree-ring dating), invented over 100 years ago by A. E. Douglass, an American scientist. This method determines the year of a cultural layer

Large saltcellar, 9½ × 3¾ × 4½ inches.

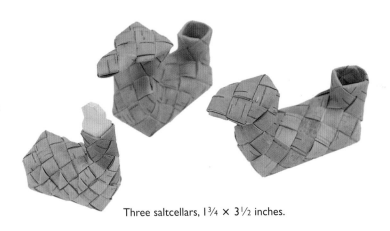

Three saltcellars, 1¾ × 3½ inches.

Saltcellar with duck-head lid, 7 × 3 × 6 inches.

Saltcellar, 4¼ × 5 inches.

Traditional Russian saltcellars recreated by Vladimir Yarish.

Canister with wooden bottom; the wooden top of the lid was stitched with some wooden pegs; thirteenth century canister and top, 3½ × 3¾ inches, recreated by Vladimir Yarish.

by analyzing the tree rings of the well-preserved roadways. Since streets were paved with logs approximately once in 17 to 20 years, and the logs were laid directly on top of the older logs, about 30 layers of logs were placed from the tenth to the fifteenth century. By studying the annual rings of the logs, archeologists can almost determine the exact year of their placement, and artifacts found at the same level can be dated accordingly.

How many birch-bark items that were excavated were made for daily use? The excavations show that they were many and varied.

According to archeologists, the ratio of articles made from whole sheets of birch bark to those woven from strips is about 85 to 15. They base this evaluation on the number of fragments found, but their conclusions may differ in a few years as new birch-bark exponents appear.

Canister with biting design on top part of lid, stitched with the inner bark of the linden tree, 4¼ × 4 inches. Recreated by Vladimir Yarish.

FOOTWEAR
- boots
- high-top boots
- *lapti* ("bast shoes")
- *stelki* ("insoles") and *zadniki* ("backs of footwear"), used mainly in medieval Novgorod
- *stupni* (similar to galoshes)

CLOTHING
- hats
- jackets
- raincoats

MUSICAL INSTRUMENTS
- horn-type pipe
- shepherd's horn

MILITARY ACCESSORIES & HUNTING
- hunting decoy
- kayak (birch-bark boat)
- quivers for arrows
- wrapping the frame of an archery bow to strengthen it

DWELLINGS & CONSTRUCTION
- roofing insulating material
- wrapping log parts to prevent decay when driven into the ground

MEDICINE
- buds of tree blossoms, used to prevent colds
- tar, antiseptic for healing wounds of cattle

DRINKS
- birch sap, as a natural tasty drink and for making beer

RITUALS
- secondary use in ancient ceremonies and customs: bast shoes, saltcellars
- tree worship in ceremonies and holidays

MISCELLANEOUS ARTICLES
- bags
- balls for games
- baskets
- bookcases
- bowls of various sizes, shapes, and uses
- bowls under millstones for grinding grain
- boxes for storage
- branches for the Russian bath
- buckets
- *bukarashnitsi* ("containers for storing and carrying fishing worms")
- clay pots, woven protective case
- coil for loom-weaving thread shuttles
- cords
- fire-lighting material for stoves or outdoor fires
- firewood
- fishing tackle: floats (corks), sinkers
- glass bottles, woven protective carrying case
- handles for knives
- *kovshi* ("ladles"; *kovsh,* singular; *kovshi,* plural), *cherpaki* ("ladles," "scoops")
- *lopatochniki* ("covers for wooden or stone grinder to sharpen the blade while mowing grass")
- *lozhechniki* ("boxes for storing spoons")
- *lukoshki* ("woven storage baskets for products such as eggs")
- mats for stove benches and other uses
- muzzles for calves
- paints
- paper for letters, books, and ancient scrolls
- saltcellars (many duck-shaped)
- *sevalki* ("large baskets for scattering grain")
- *sharkunki* ("rattles")
- shoulder baskets for carrying heavy weight
- sieve for sifting
- snuffbox
- spoons
- starling houses (small houses for birds)
- strap for connecting wooden parts
- supports, straps, struts, or other adaptations for carrying heavy weight, like a backpack
- tar, as a lubricant
- *tuesi* ("vessels for liquids") from *skolotni* ("birch-bark cylinders removed from trees in one piece")
- vessels for boiling water and cooking meals by using heated stones dropped into water or food
- walking canes from birch-bark sheets and wooden canes strengthened with birch weaving
- washstands (Suspended above the washstand, the woven birch-bark vessel filled with water can be pulled by a string to pour water into the bowl.)
- woven bottle-shaped vessels for storage of consumable products

chapter three

Harvesting Birch Bark and Roots

Because of our awareness of the importance of ecology, harvesting birch bark often triggers disputes over the question: Does removing the bark or cortex kill the tree or does the tree continue to grow? The majority of people are more inclined to condemn than to indulge birch-bark artisans for harvesting their raw material.

In any case, cutting inscriptions on the trunks of living trees, stripping the bark without special care, or any other destruction of a tree evokes a negative response from people. Therefore, harvesting birch bark to be used in basketry raises many questions, and the usual harvesting of the same birch for firewood for kindling furnaces seems to be viewed less unfavorably. These attitudes persist despite the fact that in the first case, harvesting bark only, the tree lives and continues its valuable existence, but in the case of firewood, it perishes forever.

The trunk of the birch tree is made up of the bark, the cambium, and wood pulp. Birch bark is a dense bark, consisting of many fine layers, like paper. In northwest Russia, it has an average thickness of 1.5 to 2 mm. The cambium is thicker, more fragile, and dark brown, similar to the bark of the cork tree. The cambium is located between the bark and the wood pulp. If the cambium is not damaged in stripping the bark, the birch tree does not die. Bark grows again where it was removed, and the new layer can be removed again. The second growth of birch bark is rougher than the first and resembles grainy leather. Usually the concept of birch bark includes the white part of the bark together with the cambium, so the bark of the birch tree is thought to have two layers.

If we harvest the bark carefully, without damage to the cambium, the tree will not perish, but will begin to grow more slowly, and the wood will become harder.

In Russia people have never regarded harvesting birch trees for firewood as an uneconomical waste of natural resources. Many, many trees are cut down to meet today's firewood demand. As in the past, birch wood is essentially used for heating wooden houses all over Russia. The constant need for birch firewood is compensated by the exceptional vitality of this species of tree. Birch is like a weed; no matter how much it is cut down, it grows and grows.

The timing of the birch-bark harvest is important, however. It is best to remove it from the tree at the most favorable time of the year, when the tree itself "gives up" the outer bark. This period begins at the end of May and lasts about a month, but it is not

Mixed deciduous forest of birch, aspen, and alder trees.

necessarily the same year after year. Sometimes the best period for harvesting in the Novgorod region is the beginning of June, or in the occasionally very cold year, even to the middle of June. At around the beginning of July, the tree becomes increasingly less willing to give up its bark. This special feature of birch is identical in all regions.

So far, I have not found Novgorod craftspeople who have had omens or popular beliefs connected to harvesting birch bark. In my own experience, I know that the bark is "ready" for harvesting when many gnats or mosquitoes appear.

A suitable location is needed to harvest quality material. The birch-bark artisan in the Novgorod region searches for the mixed deciduous forest where the birch lies next to aspen and alder trees. The birch bark is not as clean, smooth, or suitable for weaving where the birch trees are mixed in with too many fir and pine trees. The bark is somewhat better when the mixed forest is located in a lower area closer to a swamp than in higher elevations. In the mixed forest, the birch branches turn toward the light, clearing the trunk of the lower branches and making it accessible and suitable for removing the outer bark. When the tree grows in a birch forest where only other birches grow, it is not as tall and has branches close to each other and the ground, making it difficult to harvest the bark.

For woven articles, the peasants of northern Russia harvested birch bark solely by the strip method. With this technique, preliminary spiral cuts were never made on the tree trunk; instead, they obtained the desired width of the strips during removal of the bark with the aid of its tensile stress and its angle to the trunk.

The craftsperson usually removed a strip from the tree from right to left in a downward direction and regulated its width at the beginning as well as throughout stripping.

To learn to remove a strip from the tree in this fashion is not easy. You must try time and time again until you succeed. But the results are worth the effort. If the trunk of the tree is smooth, it is possible to remove a strip at least 33 feet (10 m) long.

In the forest, the strips are rolled up with the white side facing out. Strip after strip is rolled up, reaching the size of a soccer ball or larger.

A master can make at least 50 birch-bark rolls in a season. Winding the strip into a roll also requires skill and can be very difficult the first time it is attempted.

The birch-bark rolls are similar to birds' nests with the opening in the center. This method of rolling the bark is convenient for storage. The rolls were stored in a dry place in the barn where they could hang on the wall or lie in the loft.

Craftsman with birch-bark rolls.

The birch bark is generally taken from trees of average age with a diameter of 6 to 10 inches (15 to 25 cm). Since ancient times, Russian craftsmen have harvested birch bark in different ways depending upon its future use.

When birch bark was stored in rolls in the barn, strips were selected for weaving based on the width and thickness of the intended article. Each strip was evened out after this, meaning that it was cut from both sides with a knife and was cleaned from the top (from the white side). Any growth or unevenness was cut off in the cleaning. The craftsmen (typically men) eyeballed the width in trimming the strips; it didn't matter if they were a little wider or narrower. In order to cut a long strip, the craftsman held one end with the heel of his foot on the floor, held the other end in his left hand, and with the right

hand, which held a sharp knife, went along the right edge of the strip, cutting off rough irregularities. The strip was held in the left hand with the inner side of the bark upward. As each cut was made, the craftsman moved the strip farther along, pressing the next section needing trimming with the heel. The other side of the strip was cut after that. Frequently, the craftsman cut several rolls at one time. Then, after trimming and after cleaning the strips, the roll was wound again for storage.

After trimming, the strips were laid out according to the length needed for the intended project. Novgorod peasants used vegetable oil, lard, soap, or simply water to keep the birch-bark strips slippery during weaving. It was extremely rare that the peasants didn't use anything to lubricate the birch bark before weaving. I have met two masters in the Demyansk region of Novgorod Province who wove, as the saying goes, "bone-dry." If birch-bark strips prepared several years earlier become dry and begin to break, they are soaked in water. Currently the practice of birch-bark weavers in Velikiy Novgorod, as in my studio, is to use ordinary sunflower oil intended for cooking. It is the most convenient lubricant for the contemporary urban craftsperson.

Birch bark is stored in sheets for the production of tar and for making household utensils and other articles that are not woven. Even in the nineteenth century in Russia, sheet birch bark was freely sold in the markets by the pood (1 pood equals 36 pounds or 16.2 kg) for the distillation of tar and by a hundred sheets for making various articles.

Before the bark is removed from the tree, it is necessary to test it for its suitability to the anticipated project. It is possible to cut off

Before the bark is pulled from the tree, it needs to be tested to see if it is suitable for the planned project.

If the material is suitable, a lengthwise slit is made through the outer layer of bark along the trunk with a knife. From both ends of this slit, it is possible to make two small transverse cuts.

One edge of the birch bark is easily removed from the tree along the lengthwise slit with a knife.

After grabbing the ends of the peeled bark, the artisan can remove the entire sheet from the trunk. As a rule, the bark flies off the tree with a cracking sound, as if the tree is paying an everlasting tribute to the artisans.

The bark is placed in sacks. Wide sheets may be torn into smaller ones to fit into them. Frequently, the craftsmen roll several long sheets of bark into cylinders along the lenticle (the aggregation of cells that look like dashes on the bark), with the white side inward, and then store them this way.

a small strip of bark to see its color. The best bark is yellow or yellow-brown. If the bark is red, dark brown, or shades close to them, it is better not to remove it, since it will dry out rapidly. Then it will become brittle, break, and be hardly suitable for working. This kind of bark does not stay preserved for a long time. The tip of the strip should be bent and inspected to see if it separates into thin layers. Bark that divides into layers is less appropriate for working, because it will be constantly splitting into layers during weaving.

When they get home, the craftsmen divide the birch bark into layers of the necessary thickness, sort it, and pack it for storage. In Russia, cleaned birch bark is often stored in large plastic bags or in piles under a heavy-duty press in a cool place somewhere in the barn. It is possible to store bark that has not been cleaned and to clean and cut it right before usage. During the hot days of June, the bark taken from the tree is very moist and must be dried somewhat before it is stored; if the bark is not dried, it will darken, lose its marketable appearance, and become brittle. Usually, the craftsmen don't do anything special to dry the birch bark. The bark gets dry during its cleaning and sorting. It is possible to dry it slightly in good weather right in the forest by scattering sheets on the grass for a while. It is not a good idea to go into the forest to harvest bark in rainy weather. It is almost impossible to dry out a large quantity of bark under household conditions and the bark can rot.

If the craftsman knows in advance what he intends to weave and in what quantity he needs it, he can store birch bark that is already cut in strips of a specific size in rolls of several pieces. Birch bark always has a tendency to roll spontaneously toward the side opposite from that adjoining the tree. Therefore, the cut strips are combined in piles of 20 to 30 strips, and each pile is split in half. Both halves are placed facing each other on the side with the tendency to roll up, and the parts are compactly placed together and stitched along the sides and center with thread. The especially thick, large, and even sheets are usually put aside for making articles of entire sheets as well as boxes and *tuesi* ("air-tight canisters used for storing liquids").

The more complex method of acquiring birch bark is the harvesting of *skolotni* ("birch-bark cylinders"), used for creating tuesi. Over the last 10 years, I have been unable to locate a single artisan in Novgorod province who could make tuesi according to the tradition passed down from previous generations or who could describe all the subtleties of this craft. Therefore, I've had to rely on my own experience and stories of other contemporary craftspeople in describing the harvesting of skolotni and the other materials used to make tuesi. There are several methods of removing the skolotni from the tree, and birch must be hewn in all cases. Nowadays, few artisans make these canisters because the work is so labor-intensive.

Generally, the masters in Novgorod province make no more than ten tuesi per year. Therefore, it is unnecessary to be concerned with damage to nature. Aleksandr Vladimirovich Shutikhin, a master craftsman from the Arkhangelsk Province, makes up to 600 tuesi per year using birch-bark cylinders. But this is an extremely rare case, and certainly an exception.

The best and perhaps the only suitable period for harvesting skolotni is the same as that for the rest of the bark, although skolotni are harvested in another manner. It is better

Choosing birch for skolotni requires locating a tree with a straight, long trunk with a smooth bark and few branches.

to harvest skolotni on the hottest days at the beginning of June. On those days, the outer bark comes away from the trunk with the greatest ease.

To select birch for skolotni, you need to find trees with straight, long trunks with a smooth bark and not too many branches or twigs, in order to remove as many skolotni as possible from one tree. The thickness of the trunk selected depends on the diameter of the proposed tues. It is possible to remove as many as 20 cylinders from a good tree.

Finding this birch is not easy. Sometimes you can walk through the woods for more than an hour searching for a suitable tree. Before chopping the tree, you need to verify that the bark is yellow or yellow-brown and thick enough to spread out well and tear

properly. (Birch bark with a thickness of 1 to 2 mm is very good for tuesi.) Therefore, it is necessary to cut off a small strip of bark from the lower part of the trunk to check it.

An axe, a sochalka, and a knife are needed to harvest the bark in this manner. This method of harvesting skolotni can be called "the peasant style." The well-known master from the Arkhangyelsk Province, Aleksandr Vladimirovich Shutikhin, adopted this tradition of producing tuesi from the master artisans. He sometimes removes up to 35 cylinders from one tree. Usually he can harvest up 50 skolotni (plural of *skoloten*) in four hours.

There is another method of harvesting birch-bark cylinders that is slightly different from this one. As in the first version, the tree is chopped, its branches are removed, and it is

The tree is chopped, its branches are removed, and it is cut into logs 6½ to 10 feet long. Several skolotni are taken from each log. We lift up and place the log on two tripods that are especially and quickly made for this purpose from thick branches connected to each other and that we firmly insert into the ground.

Skolotni removal must be started from the upper part of the tree, because the tree is already facing up. We measure the size of the future cylinder from this part, and from its other side, we cut a circular strip of the double-layered bark to a width of approximately 2½ inches. We use a special tool, a *sochalka,* to remove the cylinder from the log.

We carefully place the point of this tool between the wood pulp and the two layers of birch bark (the outer layer and the cambium) from the cut side of the trunk and push it all the way through to the other side of the planned skoloten. The tool is carefully cranked around the trunk, separating the bark from the wood pulp.

If this does not work, we must try several times and insert the tool in different places along the circumference until we are convinced that the bark for the future cylinder is well separated from the trunk.

It is possible to insert the tool partially at first and then increasingly deeper. After separating the bark from the wood, we remove the tool. You can use long wooden wedges instead of a sochalka. Then the future skoloten must be torn off and unwound from the trunk simply by hand. If something goes slightly wrong, you can grab the skoloten by the upper arm near the armpit and try to sharply spin it. It is also possible to turn it twice with a sling (a long towel) and, tugging on first one end and then the other, to tear away the skoloten from the wood and unwind it from the log.

The next skoloten on the same log is chosen after this, and it is removed in exactly the same manner from the upper part of the log.

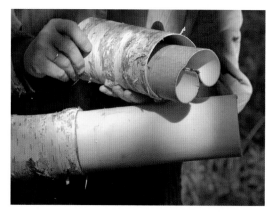

As many skolotni as possible are removed from this log.

sawn into separate *churbachki* (plural of *churback*). *Churback* is a small section of a tree trunk (a future skoloten).

Novgorod artisans have harvested skolotni using both methods shown in the photos. After harvesting, they can place the skolotni inside each other to carry them home. The skolotni can be stored for several years in a cool, dry place.

Because the tues occupies a central position in Russian birch-bark crafts, and since everyone who has experience with birch bark wants to try to make at least one tues, we will describe

Then the skolotni are removed from the remaining logs. After the skoloten is removed and released from the wood pulp, it is important to wipe any remaining juice from its internal surface with a dry rag to prevent the rapid darkening of the bark inside.

A churback should not be more than 8 to 10 inches long, or it will be difficult to remove the skoloten. The selected locations on the tree trunk for the skolotni must be flat and without twigs or any damage to the bark.

Sometimes the tool is tight, and you can try to force it to the other side. Or, with its tip, you can insert it first from one side and then from other, each time going increasingly deeper. Doing this will gradually separate the bark from the wood in a circular direction.

We carefully place the sochalka between the wood and the upper two layers (the bark and the cambium). We squeeze the tool all the way through to the wood. Then, after placing the churback on the knees (as shown in photo above), moving the sochalka along a radius of the churback, tugging the tool from one side and then from the other, we carefully rotate it around the wood, separating the upper layers of the bark together with the cambium.

We remove the sochalka after this. We hold the churback between our knees and strike it with an axe handle to knock out the wood. It is necessary to check before striking so that the bottom side of the churback (the part of the trunk closest to the ground) is located away from the blows.

Even with a short churback, one cut of the saw is wider than another, because the tree trunk becomes narrower at the top.

After turning the skoloten a bit between the palms, we free it from the cambium (the dark-brown layer of birch bark). We wipe the cylinder from within with a rag to remove the remaining juice.

We take the next churback to remove the cylinder and repeat the process. A two-man saw is used with this method of harvesting skolotni, and it is better to go into the forest in pairs.

the harvesting of other materials used in the construction of this fascinating container.

Roots of coniferous trees are used to make a tues, so we will discuss the harvesting of these roots. Novgorod artisans most frequently use fir roots. The root is used as stitching material to fasten different parts of the tues.

At first, the edges of the *rubashka* ("the external sheet of bark that wraps around the cylinder") are stitched, the cylinder-skoloten is inserted into this "shirt," and the upper and lower rims are stitched and put on the body. The entire construction of the tues is sewn with roots along the upper and lower edges. All that remains is to insert a wooden bottom and make a lid.

Roots of a coniferous tree.

Raking the ground with a grabelki.

bent. If the root's outer coating is removed, it is a little bit sticky and smells like its needles. It is slightly darker than the roots of other trees. Roots of an aspen or a mountain ash break when bent, and their aroma doesn't resemble that of coniferous trees.

The dug root must be seized with one hand, pulled from the ground with a grabelki underneath, and cut with a knife.

It is important to know that other traditional methods of constructing tuesi don't use roots or use them only rarely.

The roots of coniferous trees were also widely used in the birch-bark work of the native people of North America.

It is possible to gather roots all summer and autumn. A small garden *grabelki* (a "rake") and a knife are required. The best roots can be found on sandy or mossy ground where they tend to be even and long, but you can find them in any wooded area with at least 10 fir trees among the other trees.

The roots of coniferous trees creep closely to the surface of the ground, so their harvest does not demand great effort and special skill. To make a tues, it is better to use a root a little thinner than an ordinary pencil, but you can also use a thicker root. After choosing a suitable spot in the woods, you need to rake the ground approximately 5 feet (1.5 m) away from a tree trunk, using a garden grabelki.

Soon you will come across some roots. If aspen or an alder grow there, you will encounter their roots and these trees. To distinguish the roots of a fir tree from the roots of an aspen, a mountain ash, or an alder is easy. The roots of a fir tree do not break when

Often one root becomes tangled up with another or a third. You can leave the first root for a while, dig up the second or third root, and then return to the first one. Sometimes it is possible to gather a root at least 6½ feet (2 meters) long of nearly equal thickness; such roots are usually found in sandy soil covered with moss.

The exposed root is inside a dark-brown bark that is easiest to clean in the first day or two. The root can be wet in water and all fine shoots cut off with a knife before the bark is removed.

The external peel is removed from a root the same way as bark from a willow branch. The simplest way is to drag the roots through two large nails hammered into a stump close to each other.

Having pushed the root between the nails, you must press on the nails on top of the root with one hand and drag it with the other. In the process, the bark of the root is removed without effort. We drive two nails into the end of an old bench, and, sitting on the bench, drag the roots between these nails, removing the bark. There is also another method that can be used right in the woods. The artisan needs to cut off a branch from any birch, but preferably the same birch, about 1 1/2 inches wide and a little over a foot long, and split it in half in the middle. Then he needs to insert a root into the crevice and drag it through. The edges of the branch will clean the bark from the root. After the bark is removed, he must roll the root into a circle with a diameter of 2 to 6 inches, depending on its thickness, and dry it out.

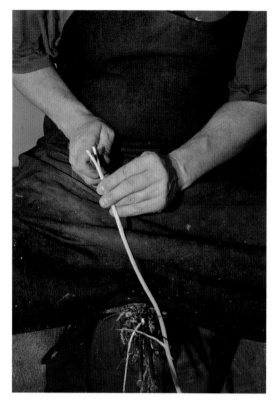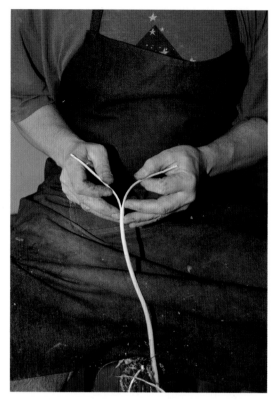

The dried root can be stored many years. Do not place a damp root in a plastic bag for a long time because it will rot. The dry root is very fragile. Before you work with it, the root should be soaked in warm water for 15 to 20 minutes, split in half lengthwise, and cut with a knife so that it is approximately the same thickness and width throughout its length. If the root is too thick, it can be divided into four parts: first divided in half, and then each half divided in half again.

Cut the root with a knife at the break and if necessary along the edges to make it more even in width throughout the entire length. The root should be damp while you are working with it; moisten it from time to time with a rag or two fingers dipped in water. When stitching an article, you need to be sure that the flat part of the root (the part that has been split and cut with a knife) is next to the birch bark.

Bottoms and lids are most often made of fir and pine boards. The bottoms are usually one centimeter or less, and the lids are always a little thicker. A willow branch the thickness of a large finger is used to make the handle. It is better to cut the branches in the early spring or the late autumn when they are most flexible. The branch is cut to the size of the intended handle and boiled in water for two to three hours. Next, the handle is bent around a prepared wooden block, a glass bottle suitable in diameter, or a can. Then the edges are fastened with a cord, and it is left to dry for four or five days.

After that, the edges of the handle are fit to the holes in the lid, the handle is inserted into the lid (as shown in the top photo on page 39), and the ends of the handle are fastened securely underneath by means of a small, crosscut stick (as shown in the bottom photo on the right).

Novgorod peasants felt that willow was not strong enough. They inserted bird cherry or mountain ash branches into the edges of their woven baskets more often than willow. The wooden handles in the Novgorod ethnographic tuesi have not yet been analyzed. Most of the museum ethnographic tuesi have no lids. Probably some of them were made from bird cherry or mountain ash. But in practice we are sure that willow is appropriate for such work.

Novgorod peasants frequently wove birch-bark saltcellars and used wooden lids or stoppers. The stoppers were usually made from wood cut from a fir tree or a linden tree, the softest and also a very widespread species of tree in Novgorod Province. Russians use the wood of the alder for them as well. It is widespread in the Novgorod area and can be cut well. They also made leather handles for small birch-bark boxes worked from sheets; woven bags and backpacks have belts made from leather.

Having prepared good birch bark and other materials, you can confidently begin work. Remember that good material is essential for a successful project.

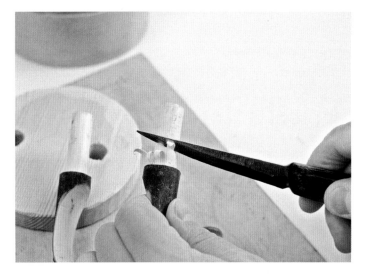

Preparing a handle for wooden lid.

chapter four

Tools for Birch-Bark Crafts in Medieval Novgorod

"Without a tool, you cannot weave a bast shoe." —Russian proverb

Artists Are Measured by Their Tools

In medieval Novgorod and the period that followed, artisans working in birch bark used various tools and materials, including awls, needles, bast fiber (bast twine), roots of coniferous trees, a kostyk, shchemyalki, a knife, paints, and brushes. According to the archeologist B. A. Kolchin, the paints used for birch-bark articles were black, red, brown, blue, and bright yellow. Making certain birch-bark articles called for special tools; for example, creating the tues required a ruler, an awl, and a compass. Modern artisans can barely manage without scissors and a pencil, but people in Novgorod villages never used them. We do not know about the tools medieval Novgorodians used for harvesting birch bark, but in the 18th to 20th centuries, an axe, a saw, a stab knife, a lopatka, and a sochilka (or sochalka) were considered standard tools for harvesting the bark.

However, certain tools and materials used in medieval Novgorod and in later centuries are familiar to all of us, so we will limit our discussion here to awls, mochalo (bast twine), needles, the kostyk, the shchemyalka, the lopatka, and the sochalka.

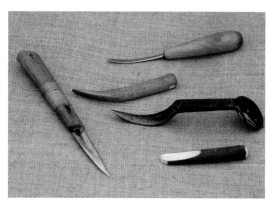

Tools for weaving birch bark: a knife, a clip (shchemyalka) and three kostyki.

Various kostyki.

Tools and Materials for Weaving and Construction

Awls

Several dozen small excavated awls with square and rhomboid cross sections are in the archeological collection of the Novgorod State Museum of History, Architecture, and Fine Arts. Researchers believe that the faceted awls were used for shoemaking and making saddles. Why would this be of interest to those who work with birch bark who already have awls with round cross sections? Native American artisans have long used triangular and rectangular awls when making birch-bark canoes sewn with roots to the hull of a boat, because these awls helped to prevent the cracking or tearing of the bark along the fibers that round awls produce. The birch-bark artist Liana Haubrich from New Hampshire also uses triangular and rectangular awls when creating birch-bark containers in the Native North American tradition. This indicates that the technique has existed since antiquity and continues to be used to this day. And we can guess that in medieval Novgorod artisans also used such faceted awls for birch bark, creating large containers for their households.

Bast Material (Mochalo)

Bast is the inner-fiber part of linden bark, and in medieval Novgorod served as the universal stitching material. Another word for bast material is mochalo. All stitched connections in birch-bark wares from that time were made with the help of cords made from mochalo. Traces of this material can be seen in many excavated fragments, and whole parts of an article that have been preserved show that they are fastened together with mochalo.

We can only guess when the use of mochalo went out of fashion in making tuesi and was superseded by roots. How did mochalo as a sewing material differ from roots? Why were roots accepted later and why do they continue to be used to this day? It is interesting that birch-bark fishing-net floats (corks), consisting of two thick sheets of birch bark approximately 5 × 5 inches in size, were sewn in medieval Novgorod not with mochalo but with roots. Therefore, roots were also used in birch-bark crafts then. Roots certainly are a more waterproof material and more suitable for producing floats than bast. Later, not only did roots take over in the manufacturing of floats but in the production of all birch-bark articles as well.

From the earliest times and into the twentieth century, rope was made from mochalo. Stitching cords made from mochalo may also have been used for stitching, fastening, or securing birch-bark products in ancient times. It is difficult to say when it fell out of use, since we do not have enough information about birch-bark articles from the sixteenth to the eighteenth century. In the nineteenth and twentieth centuries, all tuesi were sewn with roots.

Bast-fiber lapti.

Most likely, mochalo was soaked in water before being used. Certainly it was split into the desired width and steeped in water. Every artisan who has woven lapti knows that linden is soaked in water prior to use. However, they most likely did not weave lapti in medieval Novgorod, although articles were made from linden lub (linden bark) and probably steeped in water before they were used. By the way, the instructions for a *bannaya mochalka* (a "bast whisk for bathing") say, "Scald with boiling water before use." After that, the linden mochalo becomes soft and fragrant. This advice should serve us well.

Bast is quite strong. It can be used even today. It is surprising that it was totally or almost totally replaced by roots.

Needles

The fairly thin and narrow strip of bast is a thick, flexible, and elastic thread, and a needle is required for its use. Needles from the tenth century have been found in Novgorod's archeological excavations. There are too many of them to call them individual finds. Some of them look exactly like the needles used today.

In experimenting with bast, I've used the usual modern industrial "gypsy" needle that's 3 inches long and 1.5 mm thick. The interior of the eye is 3 mm long and 0.8 mm wide. Although I've found this needle quite convenient to work with, I thought that the eye was too narrow. When I carefully examined several needles in the archeological collection of the Novgorod State Museum of History, Architecture, and Fine Arts, I found exactly what I was looking for. According to the archeologist B. A. Kolchin, needles 2¾ to 4¼ inches long, with a diameter of 1.3 to 2.2 mm, were most likely used for stitching heavy fabric and for making

boots and harnesses. The eyes of these needles were round with a slightly flattened end. I've found, when working with it, that that needle size is most suitable for working with bast on birch-bark projects.

Kostyk

A *kostyk* is an instrument for weaving that resembles a curved awl with a sharp arched end and a short-handled spoon. Using it, bast (ribbons of birch, linden, lime, and elm bark) is able to pass through woven stitches. In Russia, there is a riddle about the kostyk: "What is small and humpbacked and knows all of the paths?"

The kostyk was cut from hardwood trees (apple and pear), was carved from pork or mutton bones or the bones of large-horned livestock, or was forged from iron. The Novgorod museum has a magnificent iron kostyk found in an excavation dating from the thirteenth century and one made of bone from the fifteenth century. Artisans in the Middle Ages and later regarded the kostyk as a special weaving tool. It is possible to make a modern kostyk from a blunt screwdriver, to cut one from a branch of an apple or a pear tree, or to order a copy in the traditional shape from a blacksmith. The traditional tool is about 7 inches long, and the tip, its working part, is slightly over ½ inch wide.

Kostyki. The kostyk is a traditional weaving tool.

Shchemyalka

Another tool necessary for weaving is the *shchemyalka* (or *shchemilka*), which is a branch split at one end that is used to clip birch-bark strips. A Novgorod regional dictionary includes two other definitions for the shchemyalka: a stick split at one end used for catching snakes, and a gadget used to support the kindling on a wooden or metal support to light a house. Most likely, the origin of the name is related to the tool's function of clamping or holding something in place. In Russia, modern urban artisans use everyday clothespins and sometimes paper clips as schemyalki, neither having anything to do with tradition. Usually, schemyalki were about 4 inches long and ½ inch thick.

The craftsman generally used five schemyalki in weaving a small bast basket with 6 × 6 strips. While weaving, he held the one not in use in his mouth so as not to lose it and to have it handy at the right moment.

Tools for Harvesting the Bark
Lopatka

Two rural craftsmen out of six whom I spoke with in the Novgorod area said that they use special wooden *lopatki* ("trowels") to help in harvesting birch bark. Similar tools could be made from branches cut in the woods, but it is better when a lopatka is dry and prepared in advance. In the Novgorod region, lopatki were made of birch or oak and fashioned in various sizes. They have no special name for them today in the city of Novgorod. In some regions, the lopatka was called *pazilo*, from the verb *pazit* ("to make a groove in a log in constructing houses"). You could say that a pazilo is a kind of original chisel for such work. It is interesting to note that Native Americans, in removing large, thick layers of birch bark to make a canoe or a large household item, sometimes used wooden wedges.

Sochalka

Another tool for harvesting birch bark is the *sochalka* (or *sochilka*, as it is sometimes called). It is used for removing *skolotni* ("cylinders") from the trunk of a birch tree. This tool separates the bark from the tree by forcing it between two layers of bark and the wood on logs sawn to the size of the intended skoloten. The tool is flat and 12 to 16 inches long, with a handle at the end of a metal rod. If you flatten out a steel rod with a diameter of about 6 mm so that it is 8 to 9 mm wide and 2 mm thick, round off the edges, smooth it out with a fine emery cloth, attach a strong handle to one end, and sharpen the other end of this metal rod, you will have a good sochalka. For convenience in use, it is best to make the handle about 1 inch above the blade to be able to bend the end of the rod at a right angle twice.

During the last decade in the Novgorod region, I've not been able to find a single artisan who made tuesi using skolotni, or could even describe their preparation. Therefore, it is impossible to learn from the people who live there the precise names for tools that existed in olden times. The name *sochalka* (or *sochilka*) may be from the verb *sochit* ("to remove or pull off the bark from a tree"). The root of this word, *sok* ("juice"), means "the sapwood of a tree, which is the external layer of young wood next to the bark." In northwest Russia, sometimes a wedge cut from a fir tree or a mountain ash is used in removing skolotni from birch trees.

chapter five

The Marvelous Tues

Of all the birch-bark articles, the tues (*tuesi* is the plural) is probably the most intriguing. It is a hermetically sealed birch-bark box, which is usually cylindrical, generally with a wooden bottom and lid. It was intended for the storage of milk and cream, as well as eggs, flour, salt, mushrooms, and berries. The word *tues* was probably derived from the language of the Komi people.

The tues was a very popular household item because of the characteristics of birch bark—its availability, ease in working, water resistance, and flexibility—as well as the simplicity in design of birch-bark products and their universality in terms of use. A meal in a tues remains warm, and water in a tues stays cool for a very long time. (So it effectively served as a thermos.) In addition, food kept in this canister is less subject to spoiling. The tues was therefore used very widely, from its customary use as a bucket, mug, or ladle, to a container used for churning butter from cream.

One resident of the village of Bizino near Tobolsk (once the historic capital of Siberia) in what is today Tyumen Oblast (province) told us that in the 1940s through the 1950s the people of the village would fill a tues with cream and shake it for two to three hours by walking around their cottages until butter

formed. It is also known that honey, kvass, fish roe, salted cucumbers, and other products were stored in the tues. And it is a well-known fact that in the sixteenth and seventeenth centuries, butter was sold in *berestenechki* ("birch-bark boxes") in the

Tiny canister with cylinder inside and woven decorations outside, diameter 2 inches, height 3 1/2 inches. Made by Vladimir Yarish.

Canister with weaving on the outer wall and stitched with bast (the inner bark of the linden tree), diameter 3 1/2 inches, height 2 3/4 inches. Reconstruction of thirteenth-century canister, made by Vladimir Yarish, using original body of tues (see p.9).

Inside stitched lid for canister shown to the left.

Canister stitched with bast, diameter 4 3/4 inches, height about 3 inches. Reconstruction of fourteenth-century canister, made by Vladimir Yarish, using fragment of lid from archeological dig (see p.8).

Above center: Canister, diameter 5 1/4 inches, height 8 inches, made by master artisan Victor Sorokin from town of Malay Vishera in Novgorod province.
Above right: Victor Sorokin's canister, shown without lid.

Moscow markets. Most likely these boxes were tuesi. Because of the special construction of the handle and lid, which closed very tightly, tuesi also were used to transport water and other liquids to the places where people worked in the fields the entire day.

Depending on their function and where they were used, tuesi had various forms and

design features. But in spite of their variety, almost all tuesi consisted of these parts:

• A body, composed of a hollow birch-bark cylinder, taken in one piece from the tree or made from a sheet of birch bark, and with a *rubashka* ("the outer layer," or "shirt"), a second cylinder made from an additional

Miniature fancy canister, made by Vladimir Yarish.

Three canisters, made by Vladimir Yarish.

sheet of birch bark, sewn with a root of a coniferous tree or fastened seamlessly in the manner of a *zamok* ("type of lock"). Frequently the rubashka was woven in a straight or diagonal direction, decorated with paints, or embossed with stamps. Designs on the rubashka also could be cut or scraped out with a knife or drawn with an awl.

- A birch-bark rim, which fits over the rubashka on both the upper and lower parts of the tues, strengthening it. Sometimes the rims were sewn to the body with a root of a coniferous tree, strengthening the entire construction of the tues.
- A wooden bottom, usually made from the wood of a fir, pine, or cedar tree.
- A wooden lid, made from the wood of the same species of tree.
- A handle, bent from a branch of willow, bird cherry, or mountain ash.

Over the last two hundred years, Russian peasants have made tuesi by using a *skoloten*

("birch-bark cylinder removed in one piece from a tree"). In medieval Novgorod they did not use such cylinders. To make tuesi, they took a sheet of birch bark, bent it into the shape of a cylinder, and sewed the edges together. The tuesi made by the Yakut (a people who have lived in Siberia for a very long time) were made from birch-bark sheets, sewn with horsehair, and used as containers for milk. The medieval Novgorodian tuesi, especially those made with a wooden bottom, were probably also used for liquids.

Design of the Tues Body

The body of Novgorodian tuesi from the Middle Ages was made of two cylinders. The internal cylinder was produced from a wide strip of birch bark with its lengthwise edges usually sewn together to form a cylinder; however, sometimes these edges were simply imposed against each other, overlapping. The external cylinder was made from a strip of birch bark with its edges fastened in a *zamok*.

Canister with cylinder inside and straight weaving outside shirt with split-root stitching and wooden bottom and lid, made by Vladimir Yarish.

The lid on this basket is made with a centuries-old Novgorodian technique. Made by Vladimir Yarish.

Apertures were cut into one side of the strips, and *yazychki* ("little tongues") were cut into the other. The tongues were inserted into the apertures, firmly interlocking the edges. These zamki were configured in different ways. Frequently the birch-bark ends of the sheet forming the external cylinder were also stitched. Sometimes the body was stitched through in several places by lengthwise diagonal, vertical, and other seam lines, probably for durability. This design of the body can be seen in individual artifacts from the "archeological" period, meaning the tenth to the fifteenth century.

Design of the Tues Bottom

Although the bottom of the tues generally was made of wood, birch bark also was used.

Wooden Bottom

The bottom of many tuesi was made from a wooden board fastened to the body with wooden cone-shaped *shpilki* ("nails cut with

a knife"). Wooden bottoms were used more frequently in those body designs where the external cylinder was worked in a zamok and the internal cylinder was overlapped.

Birch-Bark Bottom

With this design, the bottom consisted of several layers of birch bark, usually two, that were sewn to the body with cords of linden bark. Before being sewn, the bottom sheets were lined up with the lines running crosswise (the lenticel) and placed inside out, meaning with the two "wrong" sides facing each other. If it had three layers, the two bottom layers were placed faceup and the third nearest to the body was placed facedown.

The bottom was first trimmed in several places to position its curves correctly in relation to the body, and then sewn tightly to the body. There were likely several methods of sewing the bottom to the body. One seam that I have been able to reconstruct is "bilinear"; the linden bark cord simultaneously can sew

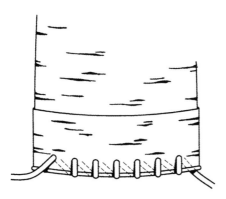

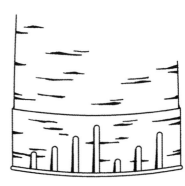

If this kind of seam is used to sew the bottom to the body of the canister, the birch bark can split along the line of stitching.

This second line of the seam doesn't sew the bottom to the body but keeps the body from splitting along the sewing line (the first part of the seam), because the holes are different distances from the bottom. This second line resembles stairs because each hole is a greater distance from the bottom in a series of four steps.

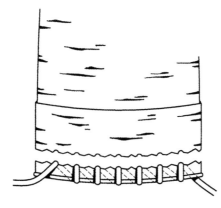

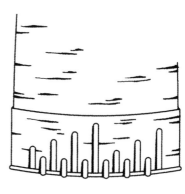

To prevent the seam from splitting, Novgorodians invented the "bilinear" seam. They added the second stair-step seam to keep the bark from splitting on the stitching line.

The two seams are combined here. This combination keeps the bottom part of the body from splitting along the sewing holes made in the first line of the seam.

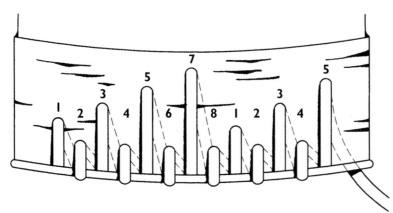

This drawing shows how the Novgorodians in medieval times could sew the bottom to the body of the canister with the same bast cord using this intricate bilinear seam. Stitches numbered 2, 4, 6, 8, 2, and so forth, are the same distance from the bottom. Stitches numbered 1, 3, 5, 7, 1, and so forth, are on different levels in a stair-step pattern. This second line is made to prevent the bark of the body along the first line of stitching from splitting.

the bottom in two ways. The first seam is a spiral equidistant from the bottom that captures the rim at the lower part of the body. The second seam is sewn in a stair-step configuration that doesn't catch the bottom but runs between the curves of the bottom and the lower part of the body. This strengthens the body by not allowing the spiral seam to tear away. The five drawings to the left illustrate this intricate seam.

Design of the Tues Lid

There were several ways of making the lid.

Wooden Lid

The first method is exactly like the first design of the bottom. The lid was made from a wooden board, to which the rim of the lid, usually composed of two strips of birch bark bent into the shape of a circle, was fastened with the help of shpilki. The diameter of the lid was a bit wider than that of the body upon which it sat.

Birch-Bark Lid, First Style

In the second lid design, in which the lid is made entirely of birch bark, the rim of the lid was slightly smaller than the lid itself and fit inside the body of the tues when it was covered. The rim was sewn with a spiral seam to the circumference of the lid, which generally consisted of two layers, or to the circumference of the lower two layers if there were three. The edges of the lid were stitched together with a long strip of birch bark that had been previously boiled in hot water to make it more elastic. This strip was wrapped around the edge of the perimeter of the lid, possibly more than one time, and was then sewn along the entire circumference of the lid with a laddered seam that zigzagged from

side to side. In two excavated fragments, I found two lids showing this method of fastening two edges together. The first fragment was dated from the eleventh to the twelfth century, and the second from the fourteenth to the fifteenth century (see page 8, photo top right, and my reconstruciton on page 45, left bottom). This is evidence that shows that such a means of lid construction was consistent among craftsmen and used over the course of several centuries. It's possible, however, that parts of the lids were not sewn with the zigzag seam. In this case, the end of the strip after it was wrapped around the edge of the lid's perimeter was bent down over the rim and hidden under the elastic strip itself on the back of the lid. (To see the inside of a stitched lid, refer back to the photo that shows this on page 45, top right.)

Birch-Bark Lid, Second Style

In this design, the rim of the lid fits on the exterior of the body. Two strips of birch bark were fastened in a crisscross manner on the upper part of the lid, or the entire upper surface of the lid was covered with strips of ordinary weaving. Probably many lids of this type of construction were made without any kind of weaving on the top, but with the surface decorated with curving lines and elements of weaving drawn on with an awl.

Is there some kind of meaning in the two crisscrossed strips of birch bark on the surface of the lid? Could it be a tribute to Christianity that was strong in Novgorod by then? Or perhaps there was something magical in the way the two strips were crisscrossed and sometimes bitten with teeth. After all, the native peoples of North America, for example, attributed a sense of magic to biting patterns in birch bark. (To see biting on lids, refer back to the photos on pages 7, left bottom; 8, left top; 10, second from top; and 20, bottom.)

Tues Exterior Design

By the twelfth century, several techniques were being used in the exterior design of tuesi (both bodies and lids), such as engraving (drawing with an awl), cutting ornamental latticework with a knife, and decorating with paints. It is possible to assume that paints were used only for the larger *koroba* ("birch-bark boxes used for storage"). There isn't a single fragment of a painted tues or *lukoshko* ("housekeeping basket") in the Novgorod State Museum of History, Architecture, and Fine Arts at this time, though some may still appear. Another technique used for the exterior design of tuesi entails using crisscrossed strips of birch bark with decorative lines made by biting the birch bark with teeth. It's difficult to tell how widely this technique was used in medieval Novgorod, because only a few fragments with biting have been found so far. The Novgorod museum has only 10 artifacts with such interesting ornamentation.

The upper part of the lid of a small tues from the thirteenth century on display at the museum is characteristic of this design technique. The lid has a diameter of 3½ inches, and there's biting in a crisscross pattern along the upper part. Some attached material also remains, as do traces of a rim that had been sewn on beneath the lid at one time. This almost completely preserved artifact undoubtedly comes from medieval Novgorod; its design features attest to that (see photo on page 8, top left).

Tuesi dating from the beginning of the eighteenth century found in villages and kept in museums were made using skolotni. Tuesi dating from earlier centuries probably could not be preserved because of numerous fires and other disasters, as well as the dearth of museums in Russia. Tuesi using skolotni are made by Russians, Karelians, Komi, Udmurts, Maris, and other groups of people living in the middle of northwest Russia, in the Volga region, in the Ural Mountains, and in Siberia.

We have no reliable sources that tell us how skolotni were gathered and used in Russia before the eighteenth century. Russian museums have no tuesi made using skolotni during the tenth to the eighteenth century. Therefore, we are unable to say when, by whom, and where in Russia skolotni (providing strong, durable, and graceful vessels for storing mainly liquid products) were used for the first time. We also do not know whether this technique for making tuesi originated in Russia or was brought from another country. Yet we can say with confidence that the artisans of medieval Novgorod (from the tenth to the fifteenth century) did not use skolotni for making tuesi, but formed them from cylinders sewn from a single sheet of birch bark. Skolotni probably began to be used in Russia later.

There is a birch-bark object dated 490 B.C. that is stored in the Norwegian city of Trondheim and made from a birch-bark cylinder. The internal part of the birch was dug out with a knife, and the remaining cylinder was used to make the vessel. The bark of the birch tree rots more slowly than its wood. Probably a tree that was beginning to rot was used in making the Norwegian skoloten, because it's almost impossible to extract fresh wood with a knife. A similar method for making articles from skolotni can be found among the Old Believers, a unique religious group in Siberia (*Transbaikalia*). The skoloten was removed from a rotten birch tree, and the decay was dug out. What remained made quite a good *vedyorko* ("pail").

Russians still used birch-bark tuesi for their original purpose, at least until the middle of the twentieth century. Sometimes it is possible to find tuesi in use today, but it is relatively rare. Seasoned by time, this sometimes richly decorated, highly artistic birch-bark article finds its place more in the contemporary world. The art of making tuesi is now primarily in the domain of urban artisans and evokes interest among collectors and experts in folk art. Newer and newer generations of skilled artisans continue to study and reconstruct medieval tuesi, strengthening their proficiency in this complex craft. (For instructions on making the tues, see project 16.)

The Old Believers

The Old Believers, or *semeiskie* ("family") as they are called in Siberia, comprise a unique regional ethnographic group. They were founded more than 300 years ago by a group of religious dissenters unwilling to accept the liturgical reforms of the seventeenth-century Russian Orthodox Church.

In 1650, the Old Believers broke away from the Russian Orthodox Church and were persecuted for their actions by the government and the church. Because of this, many devoutly religious Old Believers committed suicide. Eventually, the Old Believers divided into sects, and some fled to the borderlands while others exiled to Siberia. In 1764, Old Believers from Poland were taken into the remote areas of Transbaikalia, which is now the Buryat Republic. Scattered across the region, they lived in isolation, preserving their traditions and beliefs.

In 1971, the Russian Orthodox Church officially recognized the rites and practices of the Old Believers, whose descendants still survive and uphold many traditions of the past.

Part II

Weaving & Basketry Basics

Mastering the Craft

The weaving and basketry basics described here in chapters 6 to 8 are preliminary instructions intended to give you a good overall view of what you'll need to know to successfully create the baskets or other projects found in Part III, "Plaited Basketry Projects." Consider each of these chapters valuable practice. In chapter 6 you'll find general basket-making directions, in chapter 7 you'll learn plain-weaving, and in chapter 8 you'll perfect skills for diagonal weaving (bias plaiting).

With a good basic knowledge of plaiting techniques, you will be able to confidently weave both the plain-weave and diagonal-weave baskets. I've found that a good medium for learning the techniques is 80# drawing paper, so that you'll be comfortably familiar with making the base, sides, and any rims, tops, or embellishments when you begin to weave with birch bark or indeed another contemporary material. The paper can be used plain or painted on both sides with acrylic paint, which gives additional strength to the paper. Only one side of the paper appears in the baskets because they are double-woven, so both sides can be painted the same.

In Part IV, "Gallery of Plaited Baskets," we suggest other contemporary materials, besides birch bark, for making unique baskets (see pages 241–270). You'll also be able to view creations by contemporary basket-makers that draw on these plaiting techniques.

—Flo Hoppe

chapter six

General Basket-Making Directions

Harvesting the Bark

In most latitudes, birch bark is best harvested in early through late June because the tree is then most ready to give up the bark. Attempting to harvest the bark earlier or later can be difficult because the bark is not as readily released.

The most common method of harvesting the bark is to remove it from the tree in sheets. to do this, the craftsman uses a knife to make a vertical slit through the outer layer of the bark along the trunk. He then makes horizontal cuts from each end of this vertical slit around the tree. One edge of the birch bark can be easily pried from the tree with a knife along the vertical slit; then the whole sheet can be pulled free.

Done properly, the removal of the bark does not harm the tree.

Preparing the Bark

Bark harvested in sheets must be split into thinner layers to ensure a desirable thickness for even tension in the weaving. The strips can then be cut using a variety of methods.

Left: Both edges along the entire length are trimmed with a sharp knife.

Right: When you harvest bark by the peasant strip method, directly from trees, to remove any unevenness, scrape the white side of the strip slightly downward with a knife. Photos on pages 54 and 55 by Alexander Kudriashov, Andrey Terentiev, Alexander Belov, and Vladimir Yarish.

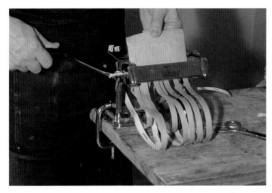

Here Vladimir uses a modern pasta cutter to cut many strips the same width. A leather stripper will do a similar job.

Vladimir also uses a rotary cutter to cut one strip at a time.

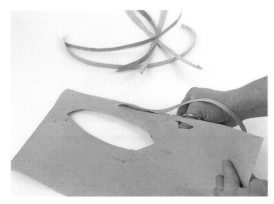

He also uses sharp scissors to cut strips as needed.

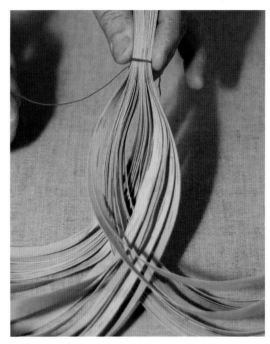

He collects his strips and pairs them up face to face and back to back, to make bundles of strips that will be used for weaving projects.

Basic Preparation for Weaving

Before the prepared strips are woven, they are rubbed with vegetable oil, pig grease, or soap and water, or simply wet with water. Each area of Russia has its own customary material for this purpose. This is done so that they will glide smoothly during the weaving. In this photo, Vladimir rubs each strip with vegetable oil.

Essential Tools

- small awl or kostyk
- scissors
- craft knife
- vegetable oil
- soft rag
- microclips

Left to right: kostyk, awl, small *shchemyalka* ("clamp"), spring clamp, knife, scissors

The right side of the weaver is the inner part of the birch bark that grows closer to the heart of the tree. It is a dark, rich color. The underside of the bark is toward the outside of the tree and is lighter in color.

Before weaving, condition all of the birch-bark weavers with vegetable oil rubbed on with a small rag.

Use microclips to hold the strips and weavers in place while weaving.

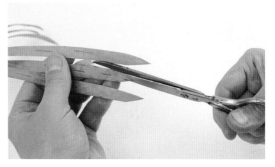

Most of the ends of the weavers are cut to a rounded point with scissors. The instructions for the individual projects indicate whether the strips are pointed at one end or both ends.

Basic Weaving Techniques
Using an Awl or Kostyk

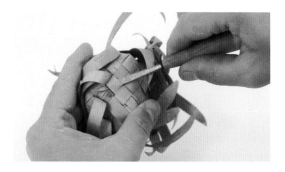

Wiggle the awl back and forth underneath a side weaver to open up a space big enough to thread a strip through.

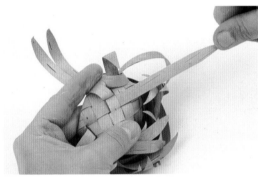

Use the awl or kostyk to help pull the strips through. Thread the strip under an intersection, and then put the awl underneath the point, holding on to the end with your thumb, to pull the strip through.

Double-Woven Construction

All baskets in this book are made using a double-woven construction. The initial part of the basket is woven with the right (dark) side up. This dark side is the inside of the basket. The weavers are turned down either at a diagonal for the diagonally plaited baskets or straight down for the plain-weave baskets. The ends are threaded through the weaving down or around the sides and across the bottom to create two complete layers. The lighter side of the birch bark is covered up completely.

Double-woven construction means that there are two woven layers, but if you look at any of the intersections of diamonds, there are four layers of bark. There are two layers of strips on the base, and the outer layer creates two more layers so there are no less than four layers of bark on the entire basket. If strips are added, there can be five or six layers—or more—at some intersections. Be sure to go under all the layers as you weave the outer layer of the basket and as you add strips.

Measuring the Strips

The length of the birch-bark strips depends on the way the bark is harvested. If it is harvested by the sheet, the length of the strips is limited to the circumference of the tree. If it is harvested using the spiral peasant method, the strips can be much longer. The most common method is harvesting by the sheet, which means additional strips may have to be added to complete a basket.

The instructions for the individual projects include both a width and a length measurement, but if your strips aren't long enough, more strips can be added to make up the overall length during the weaving. Adding a new weaver is simple: Cut one end of the new strip to a rounded point with scissors, and square-cut the other end.

Thread the pointed end under the intersection where the strip is too short (one of the side weavers), and pull it all the way through, leaving 1/8 inch (0.04 cm) extending beyond the edge.

Weave the pointed end as far as it needs to go, and trim both ends with a craft knife.

Calculating How Many Strips You'll Need

The number of weavers required for a basket depends on their length. Therefore, you may have more or fewer strips than specified for a particular project. If the basket is made with shorter pieces, more will be needed; conversely, with longer pieces, fewer will be needed.

chapter seven

Plain-Weaving Directions

The base for a plain-weave basket is woven the same as that for a diagonally plaited basket.

The difference between a plain-weave base and a diagonally plaited base is that the plain-weave base strips are considered stakes that are set up at right angles to the base and additional strips, or weavers, are needed to weave the sides and the rim.

Practicing the Technique: Plain Weaving
Plain-Weaving the Base

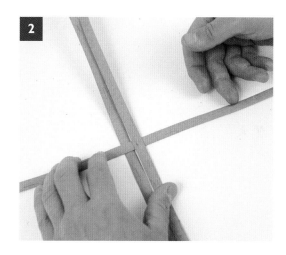

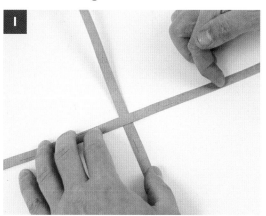

With the right (darker) side of the stake up, place the first stake vertically. Place the second stake horizontally on top of the first stake. This corner of the base is at the lower left corner and is off-center.

Alternate adding stakes in this manner—vertical, then horizontal—until the entire base is woven. (The first three photos show you the basics. If you're an experienced weaver, you may be able to take it from there. Photo 12 shows you how to square off the base.)

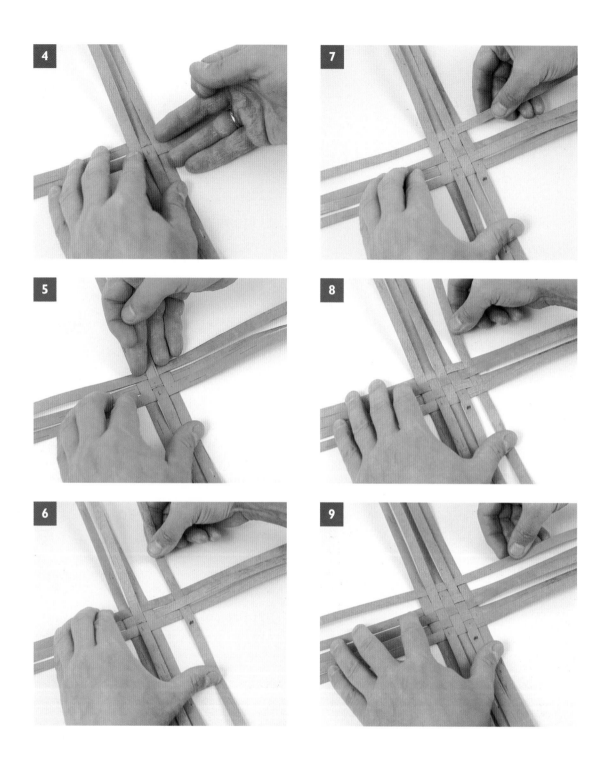

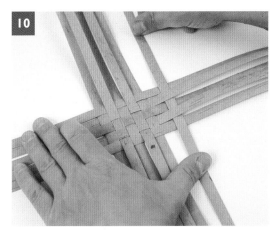

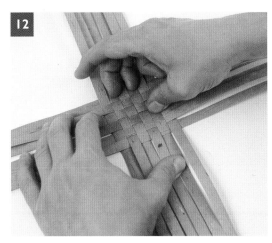

Make sure there are no holes between the stakes, and then secure the corners with microclips.

The stakes extending beyond the base on all four sides should be the same length. If there is some disparity in the length extending beyond the base, don't cut the strips off to make them even. The material is precious and any length can be used to its fullest extent.

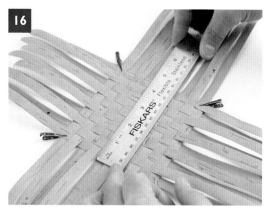

Measure the base with a ruler to make sure it is absolutely square.

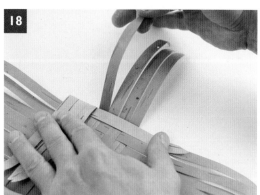

Fold the stakes at the bottom edge of the base at a 90-degree angle to make the sides. Fold one of the corner stakes over on itself (photo 17), and then fold all the stakes along the adjacent edge over it (photo 18).

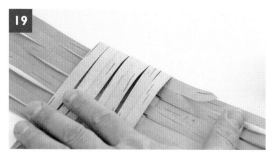

Firmly crease each stake.

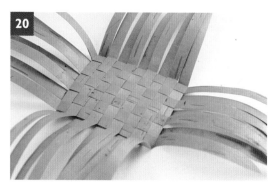

Repeat this same sequence on the other three sides.

Plain-Weaving the Sides

Starting near one corner, weave the first row in an under one, over one pattern. The first row is the opposite of the over/under pattern established on the base. Since this is a double-woven construction, each of the strips up the sides is woven with the right side facing inward.

Place the end of a weaver in front of a stake near a corner so that it will be hidden in the overlap at the end of the row.

Weave over one, under one for the entire row, ending the weaver by overlapping it for three stakes around the corner.

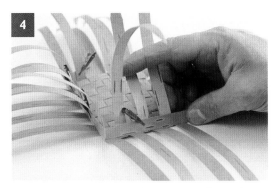

Crease the weaver at each corner so that it forms a right angle, as shown here. Use microclips every few stakes to hold the weaver in place.

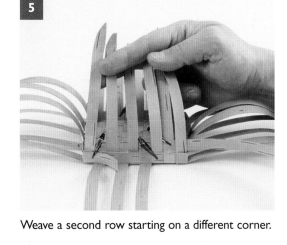

Weave a second row starting on a different corner.

End the row by overlapping the weaver for three stakes around the corner.

Plain-Weaving the Rim

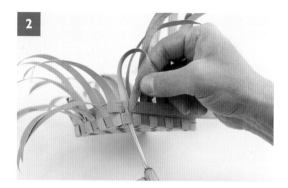

The rim consists of two additional strips that will go around the basket plus a little extra length for the overlap. Hold them together and place them on the outside of the last row.

Start at a corner, placing the outer strip at the corner and the inner strip an inch to the left, as shown in the photo.

Crease the rim pieces at each corner to form a right angle.

Fold the vertical stakes down over this rim; then thread them through the side weavers on the outside of the basket and across the bottom to make a double layer.

If the vertical stake is on the outside of the basket, fold it down over both additional rim pieces, and then thread it under the first intersection.

If the vertical stake is on the inside of the basket, fold it down between the two rim strips (only over the inner rim strip).

Pull up on the stakes as necessary as you bring them down over the rim to maintain a level edge at the top and to also make the stakes level along the edge of the base.

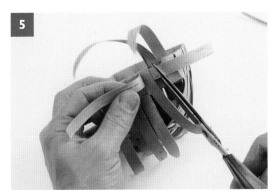

5

End the inner rim by overlapping the starting point approximately ¼ inch.

6

End the outer rim strip by overlapping it for two or more stakes around the corner.

With a craft knife, trim the end flush with the right edge of the stake.

Plain-Weaving the Outer Wall and Bottom

1

Working one strip at a time, weave each one halfway across the bottom, working from one edge. Cut the strips off, and then weave each strip from the opposite side to the middle, overlapping the ends through the same bottom weaver.

Trim each strip close to the edge of the bottom weaver with a craft knife, as shown here.

2

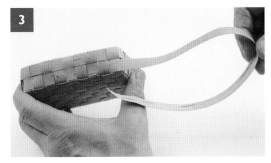

3

Weave another strip around the first row, being sure to go underneath both layers.

chapter eight

Diagonal-Weaving (Bias-Plaiting) Directions

The weaving of this basket type is on the diagonal, or bias, hence the name. The weaving elements are not broken down into stakes and weavers, because there are no additional elements other than the original ones used to lay out the base.

The corners to create the sides are woven with the existing strips either in the middle or near the middle of the base. (The instructions for the specific baskets will tell you exactly where to turn the corners.)

The finished shape of the basket can be either square or rectangular at the base and round or oval at the top.

All woven baskets in this book are double-walled. This means that first the inner basket is woven, then the rim, and last, all ends are threaded down the outside and across the bottom of the basket. If a strip runs out, add another strip so that the entire basket is finished with a second layer.

The baskets in this book have the same number of elements in each direction and an even number of elements overall. Baskets can be made with an uneven number of elements in each direction, which would create only rectangular baskets. There would still be an even number of elements overall. When baskets are made with an uneven number of elements overall, the baskets are asymmetrical.

Practicing the Technique: Diagonal Weaving (Bias Plaiting)

Diagonal-Weaving the Base

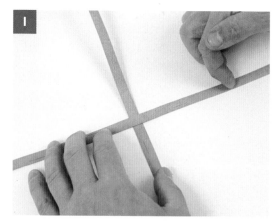

1

The base is woven with the right side of the strips up. The base weaving starts at the lower left-hand corner with a vertical strip first, and then the horizontal strip over it. (This point is critical because the placement of these first two weavers affects the weaving of the rim and any embellishments added later. All the individual basket instructions, with a few exceptions, are geared to this layout.)

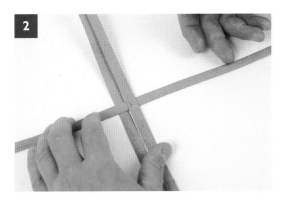

Continue weaving the base by alternately adding a vertical strip and then a horizontal strip, until the entire base is woven and the corners are held in place with microclips. (For more detailed weaving directions for the base, refer to chapter 7.)

Strips of the same length should extend beyond the woven base on all four sides. If the strips are not the same length, don't cut the strips to make them even. The material is precious, and any length can be used to its fullest extent.

Make sure the strips on the base are all very close together with no holes. Secure the corners with microclips. The finished base must be absolutely square.

After the base is woven, establish the corner points where the basket is to be turned. Count the number of weavers from two opposing corners—for example, the upper left and the lower right corners, as shown in the first drawing on the next page, the "Right Way." This forms a rectangular base (a 4-diamond × 6-diamond base). If you make the same count from each corner, the base will be square and will not weave up the sides properly, as shown in the second drawing, the "Wrong Way."

To locate the first two turning points, begin counting from the upper left corner of the base. The example is a 20-strip base (that is, 10 strips in each direction, also written as 10 × 10), which will be woven into a rectangular basket with a 4-diamond × 6-diamond base. Counting from the upper left corner, count horizontally to the right, and mark it with a microclip between weavers 4 and 5. Counting vertically from the same corner, count to the space between weavers 4 and 5, and again mark with a microclip.

Do the same thing for the opposite (lower right) corner. Count vertically up to the space between weavers 4 and 5, and mark it. Count horizontally to the left, again marking the space between weavers 4 and 5.

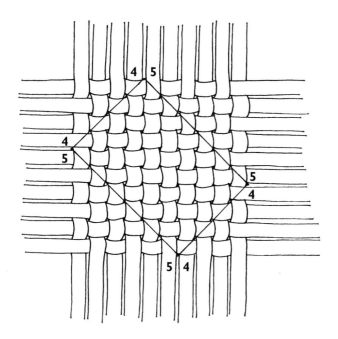

Right Way, drawn by Flo Hoppe.

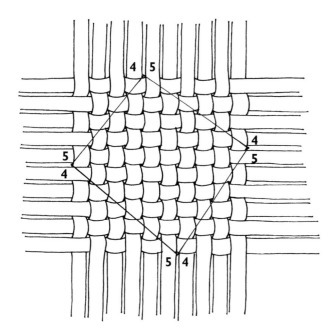

Wrong Way, drawn by Flo Hoppe.

With the right side of the base facing up, and working across the inside of the basket, make the corner by interweaving the two strips on each side of the marked space. For this number of strips on the base and the location of the corners, the left weaver goes over the right to form the corner.

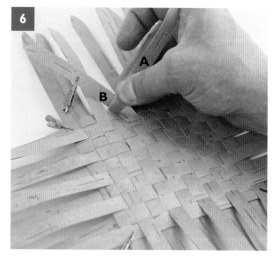

Weave strip A over strip B.

Then weave strip C under strip B, and finally weave strip D over strip A and under strip B. This creates a 4-diamond configuration. Microclip this corner to hold it in place. Weave each of the other three corners the same way.

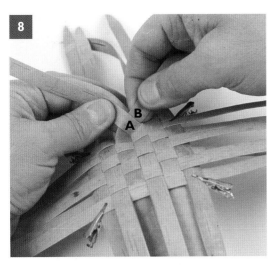

If the base is woven with six strips in each direction (a 6 × 6 base) and the corners are in the middle of the base, the right strip goes over the left to form the corners.

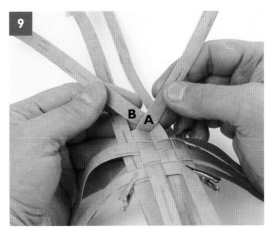

On a 4 × 4 base with the corners in the middle, the left strip goes over the right to form the corners.

Diagonal-Weaving the Sides (Inner Wall)

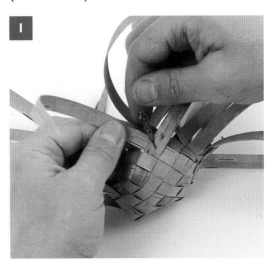

Weave the sides on the outside of the basket with the inside facing away from you. Starting between two corners when weaving a 6 × 6 base, weave one strip from the right and one from the left, and then microclip it.

Work the opposite side the same way next.
Repeat this sequence on the other two sides.

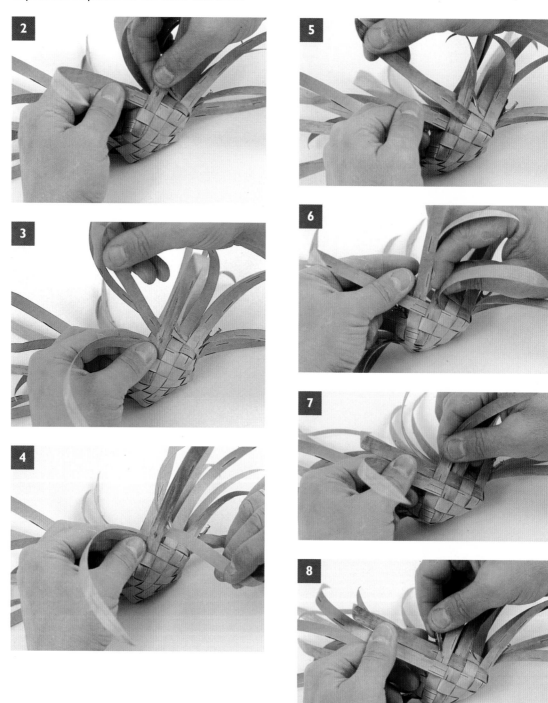

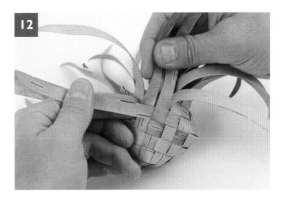

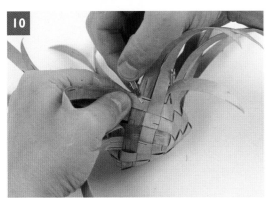

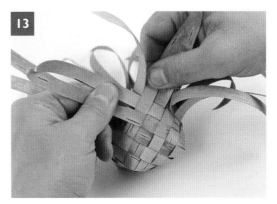

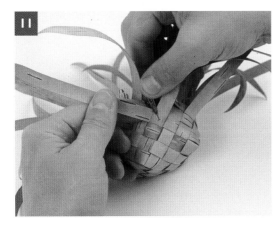

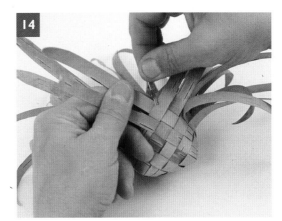

Continue this sequence of weaving the corners (shown in the first two photos) and then the opposite sides between the corners (shown in the last four).

This method generally can be applied to weaving each diagonal-plaiting project. The only difference lies in the number of strips used for the base and the shape of the foundation of the basket (either square, rectangular, or asymmetrically square).

15

16

Weave to the specified height in the instructions for the individual projects. The height is measured by how many diamonds are needed to make the desired height around the whole basket; the diamonds that are most easily counted are at a corner.

As you weave, tighten up the strips by pulling evenly on each one to make sure there are no spaces, or holes, between the strips. Good tension control comes with practice and makes a more symmetrically shaped basket.

Diagonal-Weaving the Rim

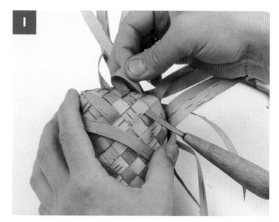

1

As you work the rim and thread the strips down the sides and bottom of the basket, the general rule is to go under all the layers. There will be places where there is only one layer, because other strips have yet to be woven in to make the two layers.

2

For proper tension and stability in the weaving, an extra row is woven above the point where the rim is to be turned. The microclips are holding the extra row in place. Don't take off the microclips or unweave the strips all at once. Take off the microclip and unweave only the two strips that you will be using to turn down the rim.

There are two methods for turning down the rim.

Turning Down the Rim, First Method

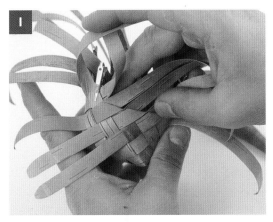

The first method for turning down the rim is to turn down at a right angle all the strips pointing in one direction (pointing left in the example), threading each of them under the first intersection.

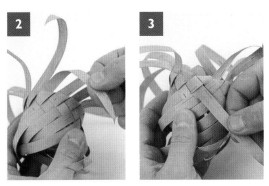

Because the remaining strips, which are pointing in the other direction (pointing right in the example in photo 2), are turned down at a right angle, each of them is threaded under only the upper layer at the first intersection (shown in photo 3). This is very important. If they are threaded under two layers at this point, the rim won't be continuous.

Turning Down the Rim, Second Method

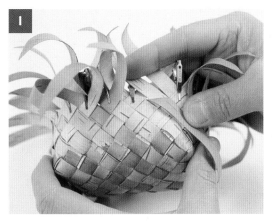

The second method is to turn down the outer strip first and then the inner one. When the strip pointing up to the right is on the outside, make a right-angle fold forward and down to the right.

Take the second strip that is pointing up to the left, and make a right-angle fold forward and down to the left.

Working to the left, fold the next right-pointing strip down over the last strip, shown in photo 3, and thread it under the first intersection under all the strips (there is a minimum of two), shown in photo 4.

Fold the left-pointing strip down next.

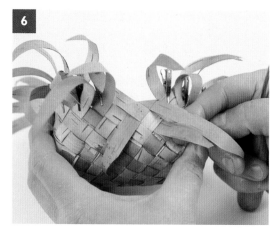

Fold the right-pointing strip down over it, and thread it under the first intersection. Continue this sequence all the way around the rim. The last left-pointing strip goes under the first turned-down strip that is pointing to the right.

The first strip is threaded under both layers of the first intersection to complete the rim.

Diagonal-Weaving the Outer Wall and Bottom

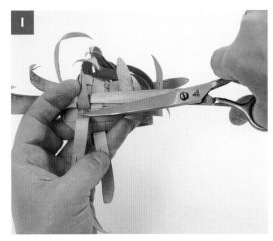

Working one strip at a time, weave down the sides and across the bottom of the basket, following the over/under weave already established by the inner wall.

When one strip runs out at the bottom, cut it off close to the edge of the intersection under which it went, as shown here.

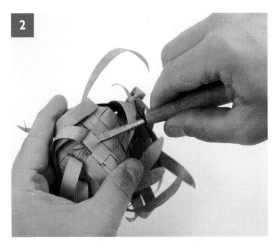

Weave the strip from the opposite direction to meet the cutoff strip, and weave it under the same intersection, threading it on top of the cutoff strip.

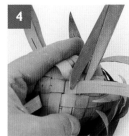

Pull it through firmly (as shown in photo 3) and cut the end off with scissors (as shown in photo 4). With a craft knife, trim the end flush with the edge of the last intersection.

If a strip is too short, cut off the pointed end and weave in another piece so that the whole base is covered.

When the entire basket is finished, use a craft knife to carefully trim off all protruding ends flush with the edge of the last intersections under which they went. Two or three light passes with the knife are better than a heavy one that might cut through the strip below.

Part III

Plaited Basketry Projects

Weaving with Birch Bark

When making models for these projects, I was reluctant to use beautiful birch bark since I realize what my co-author Vladimir Yarish had to go through to obtain it. I have searched for just the right tree(s) and harvested the bark with him.

Since creating project models requires weaving and unweaving many times to understand the complexities of the baskets, I decided to use 80# drawing paper cut into ½-inch (1.25 cm) strips to do the job. This turned out to be a wonderful idea because I was actually able to make notes and number the sequences right on the working models themselves. Later I decided to paint the paper on both sides (the same or different colors) and then run it through a pasta cutter to make ¼-inch (0.75 cm) strips. With those paper strips, I was able to make beautiful examples of each of the baskets in a scaled-down version.

Note: If you decide to do this, painting gives the paper extra strength. Be sure that the paint is very dry before you try to cut or work with the paper. When only semi-dry, the paper will be soggy and stretchy.

Over the last ten years, I have taken only three classes with Vladimir, but through those classes I did learn the basics well because Vladimir is an exacting teacher. When co-author and photographer Jim Widess took photos of Vladimir making the baskets, I observed each step and took copious notes. With the combination of my notes and Jim's photos, I was able to describe the weaving process for each of these eighteen projects. Although I am an accomplished basket maker, I had been unfamiliar with birch-bark plaiting. By not having become totally competent in birch-bark weaving before writing the step-by-step procedures, I feel that I had the mindset of a beginning student and was therefore able to see where more descriptions might be needed and where it might be necessary to adequately explain all the details and steps.

—Flo Hoppe

project one

Rectangular Tray

Weaving Level
beginner to advanced

Dimensions
base 3 1/2 × 4 1/4 inches, height 1 inch

Materials
21 birch-bark strips, 1/2 inch × 16 inches

Preparation
Rub vegetable oil on each strip with a small rag. Separate the strips into 16 stakes, three side weavers, and two rim strips. Cut the ends of each of the 16 stakes to a rounded point. Cut one end of each of the three side weavers to a rounded point.

This simple plain-weave tray is a good starting point for getting the feel of birch-bark materials and weaving. This is not a traditional Russian-style basket; it is more like those found in Scandinavian countries. Only about 5 percent of Russian birch-bark baskets are made with this plain-weave technique. This small tray can be used for trinkets. Larger sizes will accommodate rolls and fruit.

The finished rectangular tray.

WEAVING THE RECTANGULAR TRAY
Base

Weave a rectangular base with nine vertical stakes and seven horizontal stakes according to the plain-weaving general directions in chapter 7. The base measurement is 3½ × 4¼ inches. The stakes should extend approximately 5 to 6 inches beyond the base on each side. Secure the corners with microclips.

Fold all the stakes at a right angle along each side of the base. Fold a corner stake over on itself.

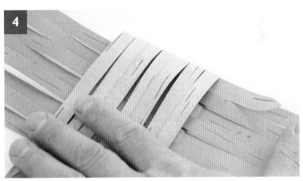

Fold all the stakes on the adjoining edge over on themselves across the folded corner stake.

The base stakes all folded and ready for weaving the sides.

Sides

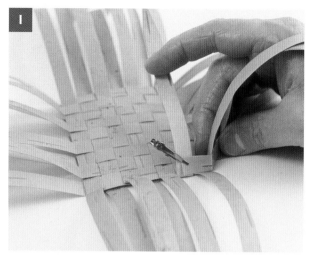

Weave the sides with the right side of the weavers facing in. Weave two rows of under/over weave, starting each row at a different corner. The first row is the opposite of the over/under pattern established on the base.

Begin the first row with the weaver in the middle of an "over" stake, as shown here. This will hide the end when you overlap at the end of the row.

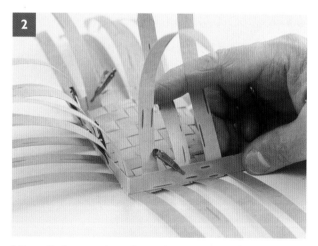

Microclip frequently to keep the weaver in place and have even tension.

Crease the weaver at each corner to make a right-angle bend. Overlap for four stakes past the corner.

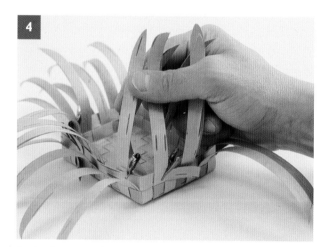

Begin the second row to the left of another corner, and complete the row the same as you did the first.

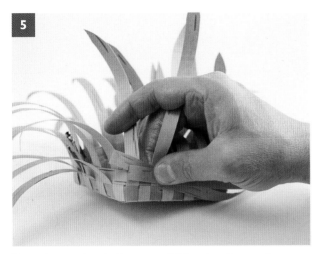

Start the rim by placing two additional strips on the outside of the last row near a corner. Place the edge of the outer strip flush with the corner and the inner strip an inch to the left.

Pull on the stakes as necessary as you bring them down over the rim strips in order to maintain a level edge at the top and to make sure the stakes are level along the edge of the base.

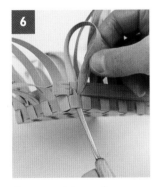 

As you get to each corner, crease the rim pieces to form a right angle. The first stake is on the outside of the basket. Fold it down over both additional rim strips, and thread it under the first row weaver.

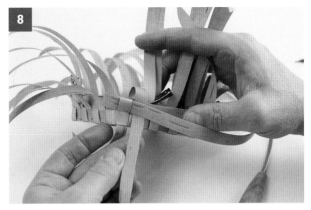

The second stake is on the inside of the basket. Fold it down over the rim between the two additional rim strips.

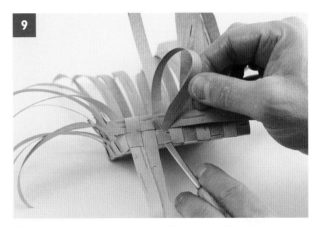

Continue working to the right, alternating these two moves.

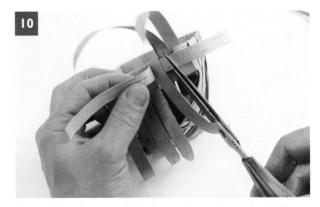

To end the rim, cut off the inner rim strip so that it butts up against the beginning end.

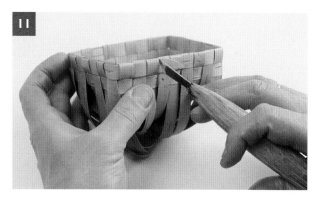

Overlap the outer rim strip around the corner for three stakes. Trim off the excess with a craft knife.

Thread each of the stakes through the side stakes and across the bottom stakes so that the basket is completely double-woven.

Trim off all the ends with a craft knife.

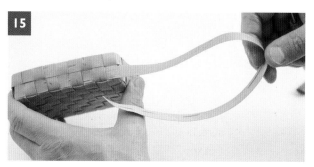

Weave a strip around the first row.

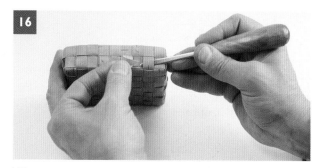

Trim the end with a craft knife close to the edge of the stake.

project two

Bottle with Wooden Top

Weaving Level
intermediate

Dimensions
base 2 inches square, height 4$\frac{1}{2}$ inches,
height with wooden top 5 inches

Materials
27 birch-bark strips, $\frac{1}{2}$ × 18 inches;
12 birch-bark strips, $\frac{1}{2}$ × 10 inches;
12 birch-bark strips, $\frac{1}{4}$ × 18 inches;
3 birch-bark strips, $\frac{1}{4}$ × 9 inches;
1 × 2$\frac{1}{4}$ inch block of basswood

Preparation
Cut birch-bark strips for the base:
four $\frac{1}{2}$-inch stakes, each 18 inches long;
five $\frac{1}{2}$-inch stakes, each 10 inches long;
six $\frac{1}{4}$-inch stakes, each 16 inches long;
one $\frac{1}{4}$-inch weaver, 10 inches long.

Cut birch-bark strips for the sides:
four $\frac{1}{2}$-inch weavers, each 18 inches long;
five $\frac{1}{2}$-inch weavers, each 10 inches long;
six $\frac{1}{4}$-inch weavers, each 18 inches long;
two $\frac{1}{4}$-inch rim pieces, each 9 inches long.

Rub vegetable oil on each strip with a
small rag. Cut both ends of each of the
strips to a rounded point (except the two
rim pieces and the weavers that will cover
the basket on the outside, which are cut
to a rounded point on just one end).

T*his is an original design using the plain-weave
technique. Most of the Russian baskets are diagonally
plaited, so the use of plain weave with different
widths of stakes and weavers is somewhat of an innovation.
The unusual shape, the carved wooden lid, and the use of
different widths of birch bark produce an interesting container
for storing small items.*

The finished bottle,
which also shows
finished chamfering.

WEAVING THE BOTTLE
Base

Weave a 5 × 5 square base, alternating the 1/4-inch stakes with the 1/2-inch stakes, as shown here. The first and last vertical and horizontal stakes are the 1/4-inch strips. The base measurement is 2⅜ inches square. Secure the corners with microclips.

Fold all the stakes at a right angle along each side of the base. Fold two corner stakes over on themselves.

Fold all the stakes on the adjoining edge over on themselves across the folded corner stake.

The base stakes all folded and ready for weaving the sides.

Sides

Begin weaving up the side with a 1/4-inch weaver with the right side of the weaver facing in. The first row is the opposite of the over/under pattern established on the base.

Begin each row two stakes to the left of a corner by placing the weaver in the middle of the "over" stake, as shown here.

Bend each weaver at a right angle at the corners.

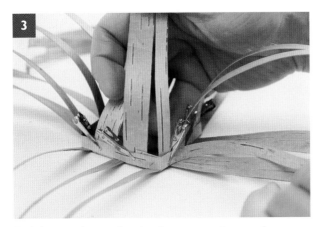

End the row by overlapping for two or three stakes past the corner.

The beginning of the second row.

Weave five rows with the ½-inch weavers. Weave the seventh row with a ¼-inch weaver.

Top

To form the inward bend at the top, fold the stakes in above the last row of side weaving. Fold each stake firmly over your awl to form a right angle.

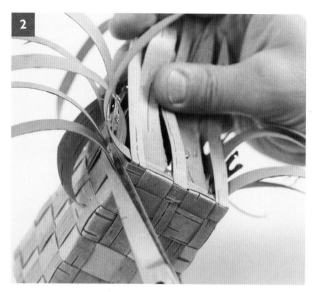

Weave the corner ¼-inch weaver on the right over to the left. Cut off the ¼-inch weaver on the left.

Then thread the weaver from the right down the side. Weave the corner ¼-inch weavers on the other three sides the same way.

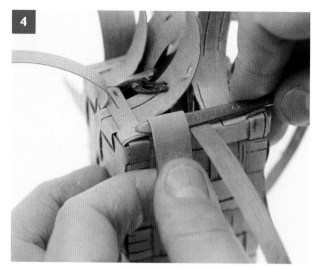

To form the straight part of the top, fold the stakes over your awl on an outward bend.

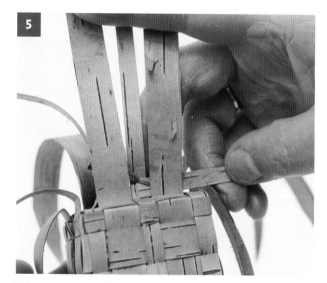

Weave a row with the ¼-inch weaver, starting over the middle stake on one side.

Rim

1

Place the two additional ¼-inch rim pieces on the outside of the last row, beginning in the middle of a side and placing the outer rim ½ inch to the right of the inner rim.

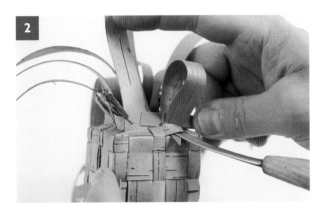

2

3

Fold the rim pieces at a right-angle bend at each corner. Fold the stakes down over the rim. The stakes inside the basket fold over the inside added rim strip only; the stakes on the outside fold over both added rim strips and are threaded through the ¼-inch weaver on the side.

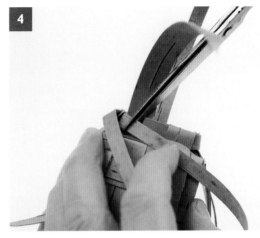

4

Butt the inner rim with the beginning.

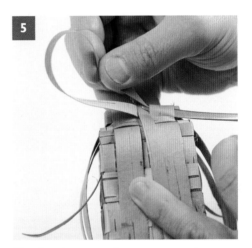

5

Overlap the outer rim over two stakes.

Outer Wall and Bottom

Thread all the stakes down the sides and across the bottom. Weave strips on each of the horizontal side rows with the right side facing out. Be sure to go underneath all layers of weaving. Trim all the ends with a craft knife.

MAKING THE WOODEN TOP

Carve the curved top out of the 1 × 2¼-inch block of basswood. Carve the square bottom part to 1½ inches square and ¼ inch deep so that it will fit snugly into the opening of the basket. Carve the top part to form a rounded curve from side to side. The other two ends are flat (photo 3).

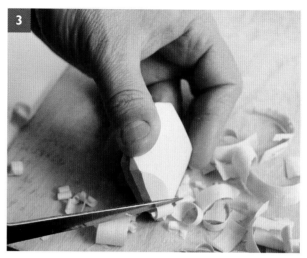

Chamfer all of the top edges and cut the corners off at an angle (see finished bottle on page 83).

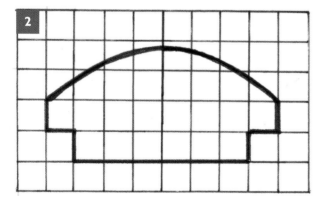

The profile of the lid resembles that in this drawing, made by Flo Hoppe.

project three

Ripples Basket

Weaving Level
intermediate

Dimensions
base 3⅝ inches square, height 2 inches

Materials
21 birch-bark strips, ⅝ × 18 inches

Preparation
Cut birch-bark strips: 12 stakes, each 18 inches long; five weavers, each 18 inches long; two rim strips, each 18 inches long; and four strips, each 6 inches long, for the embellishment. Rub vegetable oil on each strip with a small rag. Cut both ends of each of the 12 stakes to a rounded point. Cut one end of each of two weavers to a rounded point. Cut one end of each of the 6-inch strips to a rounded point.

This uniquely shaped basket is the result of Vladimir's best students wanting to create something new based on the traditional techniques he has taught them in his studio over the years. Sometimes he suggests a new idea; sometimes they suggest something to him. Vladimir sees his studio as the kitchen where they "cook" their new baskets from the ingredients that they all share.

Ripples builds on the plain-weave techniques of the first two projects. The zigzag edge along the bottom becomes a rippled edge at the top. A pinwheel embellishment on each side adds an interesting touch.

The finished basket.

89

WEAVING THE RIPPLES BASKET
Base of the Ripples Basket

Weave a 6 × 6 square base according to the plain-weaving general directions in chapter 7. The right side of the stakes is facing up, as shown here. The base measures $3\frac{5}{8}$ inches square. Secure the corners with microclips. There are two center stakes in each direction and a zigzag edge along the base between these two center stakes.

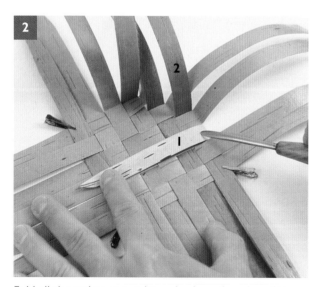

Fold all the stakes at a right angle along the edge of the base. Begin on the right side of the base by folding stake 1 back over on itself.

Fold stake 2 down over stake 1.

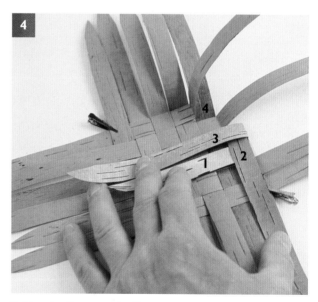

Fold stake 3 over stake 2.

Fold stake 4 down over stake 3.

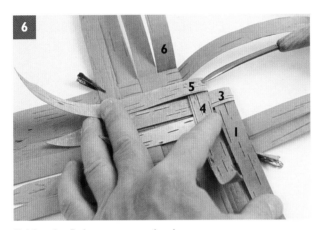

Fold stake 5 down over stake 4.

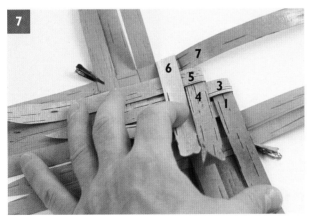

Fold stake 6 down over stake 5.

Fold stake 7 over stake 6. Work the same sequence on the other three sides.

The stakes all folded.

Sides of the Ripples Basket

Begin weaving the first row of under/over at the center two stakes on one side. Weave with the right side of the weavers facing in. The first row is the opposite of the over/under pattern established on the base.

Microclip the first weaver in front of the left center stake, right side inside, as shown here.

Microclip frequently to hold the weaver in place. Overlap the end of the weaver over three stakes at the end of the row and each subsequent row. Then trim the end.

Weave over/under around the zigzag edge of the base, making right-angle bends with the weaver at each corner, as shown in photos 2 and 3.

The base configuration at the end of the first row.

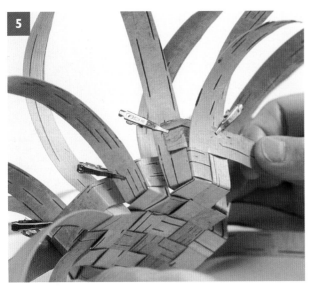

Begin the second row on the second side. Start around the corner from the left center stake, as shown here. Continue to form sharp corners.

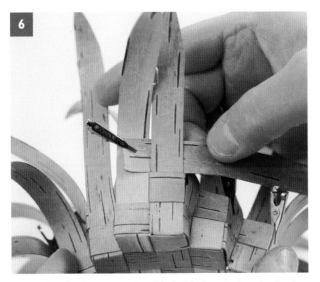

Begin the third row on the third side by placing the beginning part of the weaver on top of the left center stake.

Continue to form sharp corners.

Rim of the Ripples Basket

Starting on the fourth side, place the two additional rim strips in front of the top row, staggering the ends.

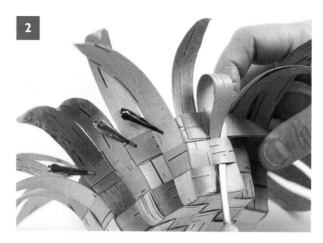

Fold each of the stakes over the rim, and thread them through the weaving on the side of the basket. The first stake is on the outside of the basket, so it folds over the two additional rim strips and threads into the first weaver, as shown in the photos above.

The next stake is on the inside of the basket, so it folds down between the two additional rim strips. The photo shows the second stake in place and the third stake being threaded into the side weaver.

Cut the inner rim off flush with the beginning end.

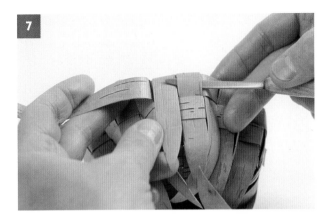

Overlap the outer rim, and thread it under the beginning of the row for three stakes.

Trim off the end.

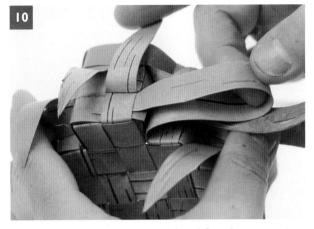

Double up the weaving in rows 1 and 2 with more strips, lifting up all the stakes coming down from the rim as you weave.

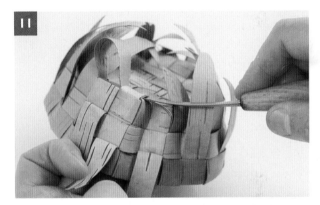

Weave all the stakes down the sides and across the bottom.

Trim all the ends with a craft knife.

Embellishment of the Ripples Basket

1

Work the pinwheel embellishment on the center two stakes and the top two rows on each side in a counter-clockwise direction.

Begin by threading a 6-inch strip, wrong side out, under square A, as shown here.

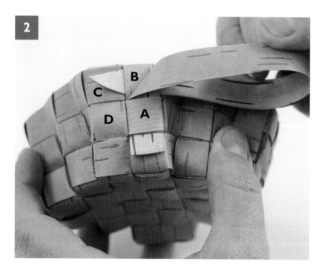

2

Fold it on a diagonal to the right, and then thread the end, wrong side out, through square B. Press the fold flat.

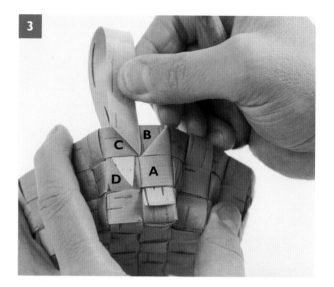

3

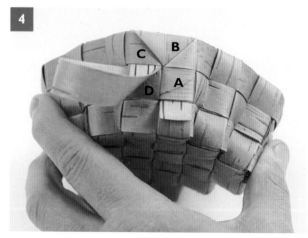

4

Continue this sequence for the next two sides of the pinwheel, folding and threading through square C (photo 3) and square D (photo 4).

5

End by threading the strip up under square A on top of the beginning end.

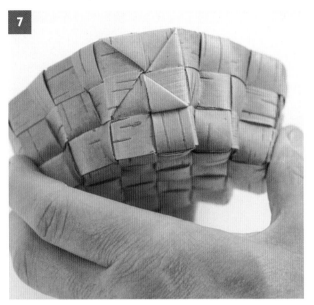

7

The finished pinwheel embellishment.

6

Trim the ends.

project four

Small Basket with Three-Part Braid

Weaving Level
beginner to advanced

Dimensions
base of finished basket 2½ inches square;
height 1¾ inches

Materials
15 birch-bark strips, ½ inch × at least
14 inches

Preparation
Rub vegetable oil on each of the strips
with a small rag. Cut both ends of each of
12 strips to a rounded point. Cut one
end of each of three strips for the braid
to a rounded point.

This basket has a square base, a round top, and a braid trim, and it's very traditional and widespread in Russia. Larger versions of this basket were used in Russian villages for many housekeeping purposes. It is an excellent beginning basket for learning the basic structure and techniques of diagonal plaiting. It can be made in many different sizes. The instructions give the dimensions and the sizes of materials to make a nesting set of three.

The completed basket with a three-part braid.

WEAVING THE SMALL BASKET
Base

The base consists of six horizontal strips and six vertical strips, as shown in the photo. Work the base according to the general basket-making directions in chapter 6. Make sure the strips are close together with no holes, and secure the corners with microclips. The base weaving before the corners are located measures 3 inches square.

Corners

The side corners are in the center of each side of the base.

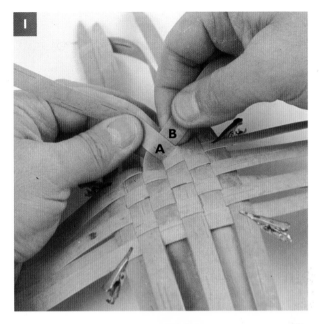

Mark the space between strips 3 and 4 on each side. With the right side of the base facing up, and working across the inside of the basket, weave strip A over strip B (photo 1) and under strip C (photo 2).

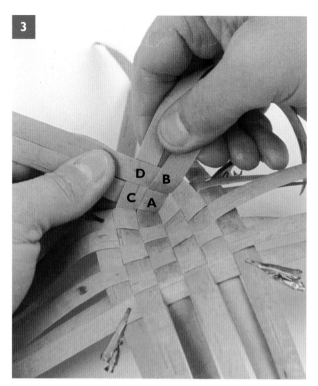

Weave strip D under strip B and over strip C.

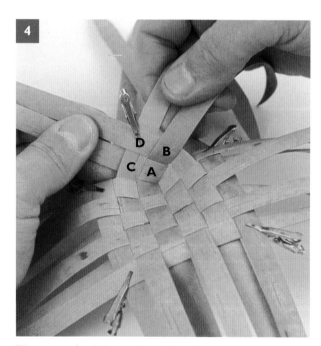

This creates a 4-diamond configuration.

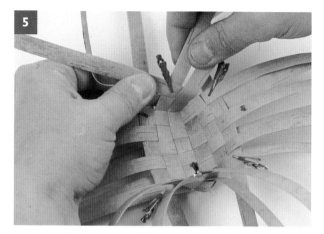

Secure with a microclip. Weave the opposite corner the same way.

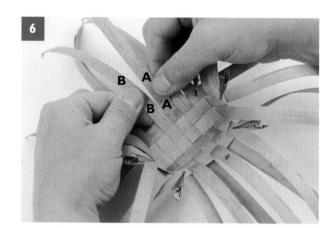

Weave the third corner the same way (photo 6), and then the opposite corner (photo 7).

Sides (Inner Wall)

1

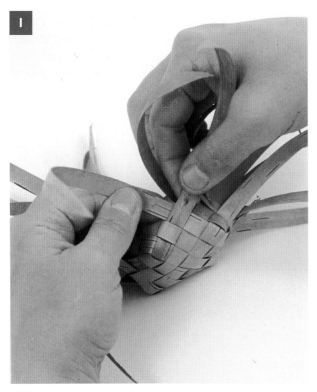

2

With the outside of the basket facing toward you, weave in between the corners by taking one strip from the left and one from the right, as shown here. Repeat this sequence on the other side, and then work the two remaining sides the same way. (For weaving the sides, refer to diagonal-plaiting directions in chapter 8. Review the step-by-step photos, from photo 1 on page 69 to photo 8 on page 70, as needed.)

At the corner, weave one strip from the left and one from the right. Repeat this sequence on the opposite corner, and then work the two remaining corners the same way. Keep weaving in this manner until you have woven three diamonds up, counting at a corner, as shown in the photo. Weave one more row for stability. (Refer to diagonal-weaving directions in chapter 8 for weaving the sides. Review photos 9 to 11 on page 71.)

Rim

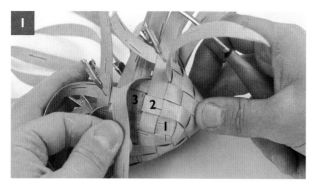

The rim starts in the middle of the third diamond up from the corner. Unweave only the two strips you are using to work the rim, as shown here.

Fold the left-pointing strip down at a right angle.

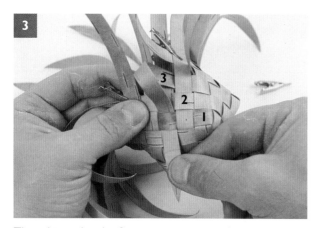

Thread it under the first intersection on the side.

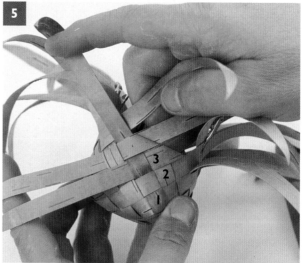

Working to the left, unweave the next two strips (photo 4) and continue the sequence of folding the left-pointing strip down at a right angle and threading it under the first intersection on the side (photo 5).

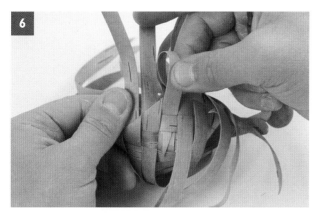

Work the entire rim this same way.

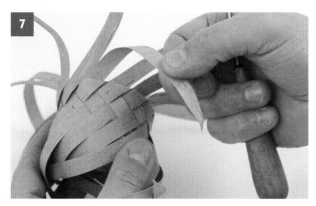

Now work with the inner strips that are pointing to the right.

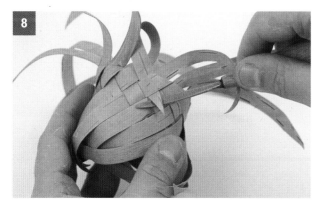

Fold each of them at a right angle, and thread them under only one layer of the first row—the layer formed by the first folded strips.

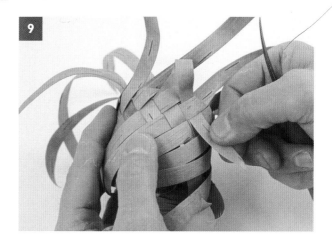

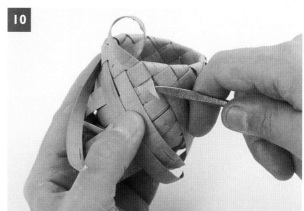

Work the rest of the rim around to the left.

Outer Wall

1

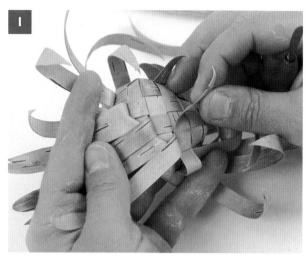

Thread each of the strips to the middle of the bottom, overlapping the strips to make sure the entire surface is covered.

2

Make sure that as you weave the strips on the outside of the basket, they go under all the layers of weaving. Trim the ends with a craft knife.

Embellishment, the Three-Part Braid

1

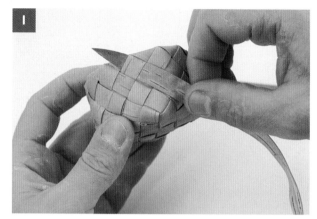

Each of the three strips makes a complete zigzag circuit of the basket, and the end threads under its own beginning.

With the underside facing out, thread one of the strips up under a diamond at the top of the basket, as shown here.

2

Pull the strip through until only ¼ inch appears at the lower edge of the diamond.

3

Working to the left, fold the strip at a right angle and thread it down under all the layers of the lower diamond.

4

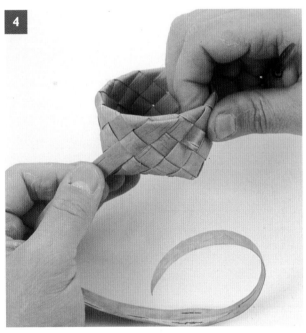

Press the fold flat.

5

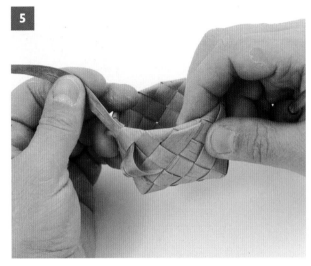

Fold the strip at a right angle and thread it up under the top diamond.

6

Press the fold flat.

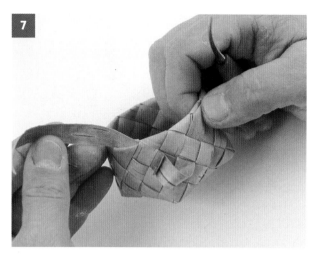

7

Make sure that you pull the braid strip down tightly to make the braid level and slightly lower than the top of the rim. Continue threading the strip in this zigzag manner for the entire row. To end, thread the strip underneath the beginning, as shown here.

8

Add the second strip up through the top diamond to the right of the first strip.

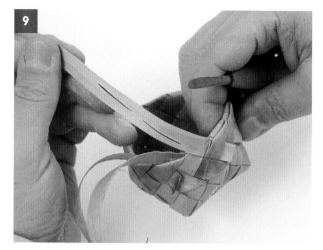

9

End the row by threading the strip underneath the beginning. Begin the third strip to the right of the second strip, as shown here, and work as you did for the last two rows.

10

Be sure to go under all layers as you thread the strips in the zigzag pattern both up and down.

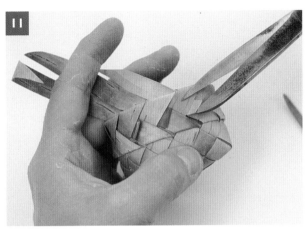

Trim all the ends. If you start the braid with the underside facing out, the top half of the braid will have the right side of the strip facing out and the lower half will have the underside of the strip facing out. If you start the braid with the right side facing out, the top half of the braid will have the underside of the strip facing out and the lower half will have the right side of the strip facing out.

FOR A NESTING SET OF THREE BASKETS

Small Basket (6 x 6 Base)
• 15 strips, each 14 inches long
• Weave two and a half diamonds high.
• The braid is worked with three separate strips started on three consecutive diamonds.

Medium-Size Basket (8 x 8 Base)
• 19 strips, each 16 inches long
• The braid is started on one diamond, and strips are added as necessary. End the braid with the strip going under its own beginning.

Large Basket (10 x 10 Base)
• 23 strips, each 18 inches long
• Weave three diamonds high.
• The braid is worked the same as for the medium-size basket.

Note: It may be necessary to have additional strips for each of the baskets to complete the outer wall and make the braid.

Two sizes of the finished basket.

project five

Oval Basket with Curls

Weaving Level
beginner to advanced

Dimensions
base of finished basket 4½ × 3¾ inches;
height 1½ inches

Materials
21 birch-bark strips, ½ inch × at least
15 inches

Preparation
Rub vegetable oil on each of the strips
with a small rag. Cut both ends of each of
the strips to a rounded point.

   In preparation for curl embellishment,
cut one strip in half lengthwise to produce
two ¼-inch strips. Cut one end of each
of these two strips to a rounded point.

*T*his oval basket with curls is a shape that contemporary birch-bark weavers in Novgorod like to make today. This is another good beginning basket that is made with the basic diagonal-plaiting techniques. If it is made on a large scale, it can be used for fruit or muffins. The smaller version can hold things like nuts or trinkets.

The finished oval basket with curls.

WEAVING THE OVAL BASKET
Base

Weave a square base with 10 vertical and 10 horizontal strips with the right side up, according to the diagonal-weaving (bias-plaiting) general directions in chapter 8. Make sure the strips are close together with no holes, and secure the corners with microclips.

The base weaving before the corners are located measures 4¹/₂ inches square. Make sure the base is absolutely square.

Side Corners

To locate the first two side corner points, start counting from the lower right corner. Counting horizontally to the left, mark the space between strips 4 and 5 with a micro-clip. Counting up vertically from the same corner, mark the space between strips 4 and 5.

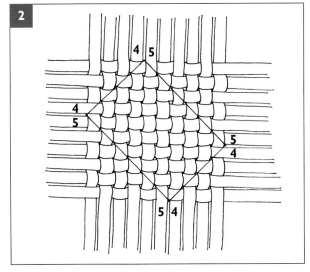

Do the same thing for the upper left corner, counting down vertically to the space between strips 4 and 5, and then over horizontally to the space between strips 4 and 5. This involved counting method produces a symmetrical rectangular base, as shown in this drawing by Flo Hoppe.

With the right side of the base facing up, and working across the inside of the basket, weave strip A over strip B.

Do the same with the other three corners. The photo shows the four corners turned up.

Go to the outside of the basket, and weave strip C over strip B and under strip D.

Put a microclip at the top of this 4-diamond configuration to secure it. Weave the other three corners the same way.

Sides (Inner Wall)

With the outside of the basket facing you, weave the sides up to three diamonds high. It is easiest to count the diamonds at the corners. Make sure the height of the basket is the same all the way around.

Rim

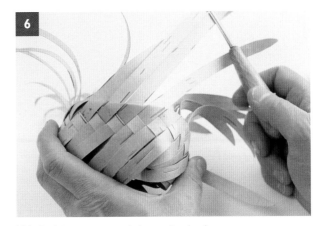

In photo 9, the awl points to the first strip that will be turned down for the rim. The strip is marked with an X. Fold this outer left-pointing strip down at a right angle, and thread it under the first intersection on the side, as shown in photos 1 through 3.

Working to the left, unweave the next two strips, and fold the left-pointing strip at a right angle, threading it under the first intersection.

Work this way around the entire basket.

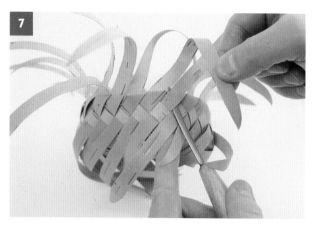

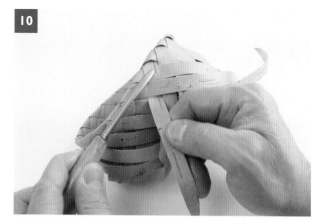

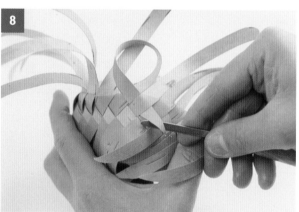

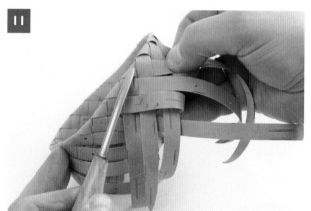

Now work the inner strips that are pointing to the right (photo 7). Working to the left, fold each of them down at a right angle, and thread them under only one layer—the layer formed by the first folded strip.

After the rim is complete, pull each strip snug to make the edge of the rim even and tight. Photo 12 shows the completed rim.

Outer Wall

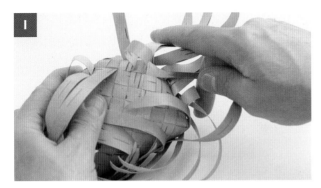

Thread each of the strips in one direction down to the middle of the bottom.

Thread the strips from the opposite direction, and overlap the ends on the bottom.

If you need to add a strip to make the double layer complete on all the strips, cut a short strip to a rounded point and thread it under the weaver on the basket that needs the extra length.

Trim both ends of the added strip with a craft knife.

CURL EMBELLISHMENT

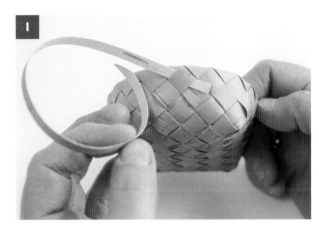

With the underside facing up, thread the 1/4-inch strip under a diamond that points up to the right at the top of the basket.

Working to the left, thread it under the next diamond, again with the underside facing up.

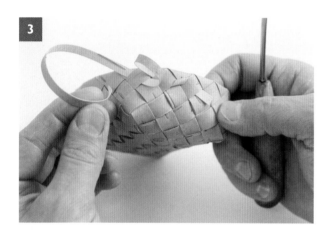

Pull the strip snug (photo 3), and flatten the curl with your awl (photo 4).

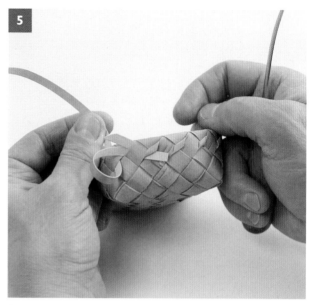

Add a new strip by overlapping the ends.

Overlap the final end under the beginning, and trim both ends with a craft knife.

project six

Bottle with Stopper

Weaving Level
beginner to advanced

Dimensions
base of finished basket 1½ inches square; height 3¼ inches; height with stopper 4½ inches

Materials
10 birch-bark strips, ½ inch × at least 16 inches; 1 × 2 inch block of basswood

Preparation
Rub vegetable oil on each of the strips with a small rag. Cut both ends of each of the strips to a rounded point.

This kind of bottle shape is very traditional and widespread in Russia where people use birch bark for weaving. Peasants used these bottles for storing grain, seeds, dried peas, dried fruits, and other items. This shape can be made in larger sizes in either of two ways—by using wider strips or by using a greater number of strips.

The finished bottle, and the stopper sitting beside it.

115

WEAVING THE BOTTLE
Base

The base consists of four horizontal strips and four vertical strips. Work the base according to the general basket-making directions in chapter 6. Make sure the strips are close together with no holes, and secure the corners with microclips. The base weaving before the corners are located measures 2 inches square. Make sure the base is absolutely square. Microclip the corners of the base.

Side Corners

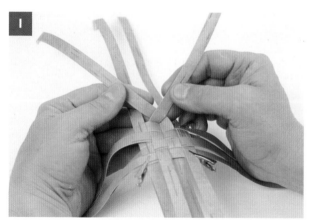

The side corners are located in the middle of each side. Weave all four corners by first taking the left strip over the right, as shown here. Weave a 4-diamond corner on each side from the inside.

The first completed corner with microclips.

Sides

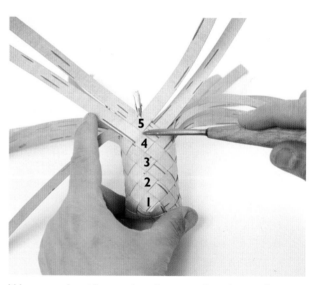

Weave up the sides so that there are five diamonds up from the corners and the outside strips are pointing to the right. The fifth row creates an additional row for stability.

Shoulders

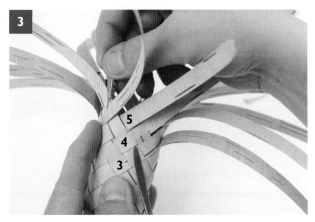

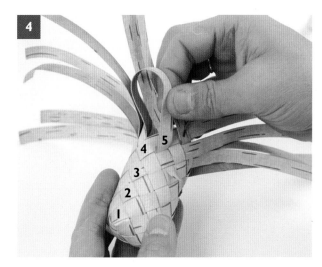

The awl in photo 1 points to where one of the shoulders is turned. Cut off the strip marked with an X to the right of the fourth diamond. Microclip the two strips to the left (photo 3).

With the underside up, thread strip 5 on top of the cutoff strip (photo 4). This forms one shoulder (photo 5).

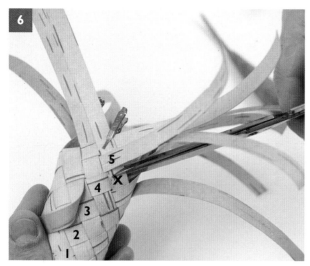

6

Go to the next corner and cut off strip X for the second shoulder.

8

Work shoulders 3 and 4 the same way. Thread each of the strips forming the shoulders halfway down the sides of the basket.

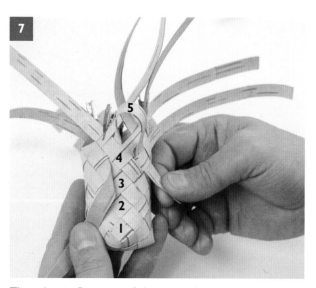

7

Thread strip 5 on top of the cut end.

Neck

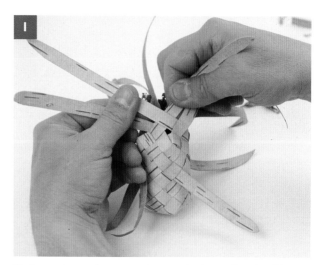

1

To form the neck, weave the strips above the shoulders.

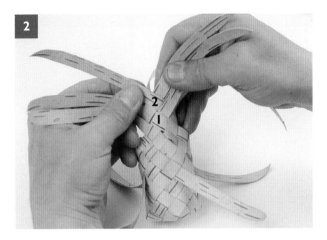

Pull each of the strips tight so that there are no holes between them.

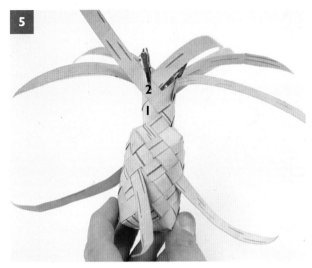

Weave two diamonds up all the way around so that all the outside strips point to the left, as shown here. Pull on the ends of each of the strips to make sure there are no holes.

Rim

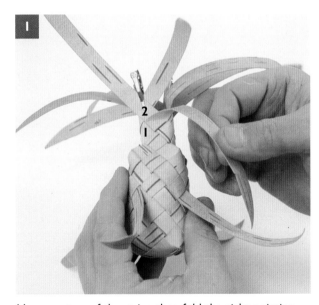

Unweave two of the strips; then fold the right-pointing strip down at a right angle.

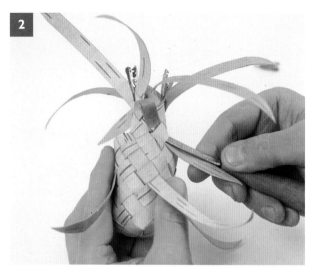

Thread it through the first intersection on the side. The height of the neck at this point is one diamond high.

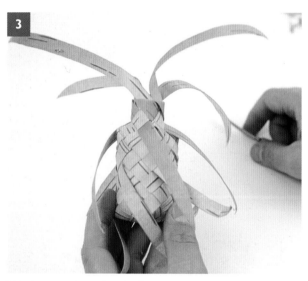

Working to the right, do the same thing with each of the next three strips.

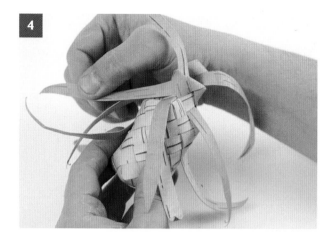

Next, working to the left, fold each of the inner strips that are pointing to the left at a right angle, threading them under only the one layer that is formed by the first rim strips.

The completed rim is square when viewed from the top.

Completing the Basket

1

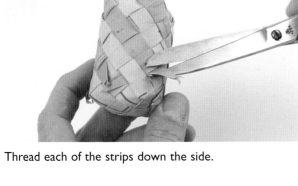

Thread each of the strips down the side.

2

3

4

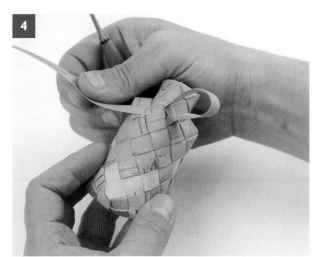

5

6

7

Keep adding more strips as needed to completely cover the basket with a second layer (photos 2–7).

8

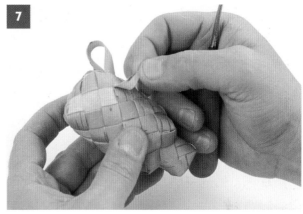

Trim all the ends.

MAKING THE STOPPER

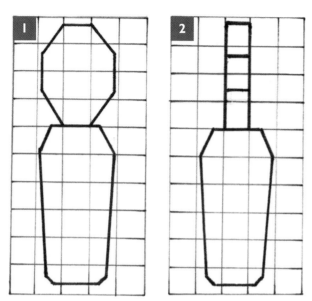

From a 1 × 2 inch block of basswood, carve the stopper, as shown in drawing 1. The opening of the bottle is ⅝ inch square. Carve the bottom of the stopper on a taper from ½ inch at the bottom to ⅝ inch at the widest point 1 inch up. Carve an eight-sided top ¼ inch deep. Chamfer all the edges. Drawing 2 shows a side view of the stopper. Drawings by Flo Hoppe.

The finished bottle with the stopper in place.

project seven

Saltcellar

Weaving Level
intermediate to advanced

Dimensions
base of finished saltcellar 1 1/2 inches × 3/4 inch; height 2 3/8 inches; height with stopper 3 1/4 inches

Materials
eight birch-bark strips, 1/2 inch × 16 1/2 inches

Preparation
Rub vegetable oil on each of the strips with a small rag. Cut both ends of each of six strips to a rounded point. Cut one end of each of two strips to a rounded point for the pinwheel embellishments.

B irch-bark salt containers can be found in many different sizes and shapes in Russia and in Scandinavian countries. This one is a traditional peasant's saltcellar. Salt was a precious commodity, and peasants used this type of container to store it when working or traveling. The construction of this basket involves several of the techniques learned in project 6, *Bottle with a Stopper.*

Finished saltcellar with stopper.

WEAVING THE SALTCELLAR
Saltcellar Base

The base consists of three horizontal strips and three vertical strips (shown here). Work the base according to the general basket-making directions in chapter 6. Make sure the strips are close together with no holes, and secure the corners with microclips. The base weaving measures 1 ⅜ inches square. Make sure the base is absolutely square.

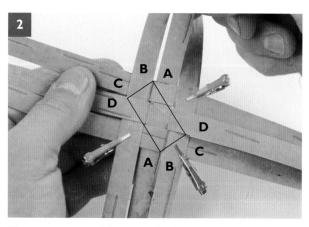

This is a very small base, so the first and second side corners are woven at the same time. The first two corners are at the upper left base corner (shown in the photo) and are located between strips 1 and 2 both horizontally and vertically.

With the right side of the base facing up, and working across the inside of the basket, weave strip A over strip B.

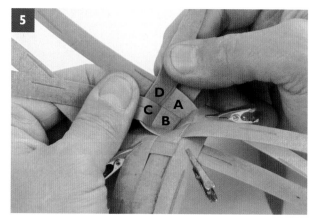

Weave strip C over strip D (photo 4) and strip D over strip A (photo 5).

Saltcellar Sides (Inner Wall)

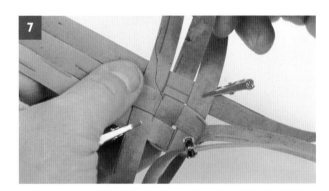

Microclip this 4-diamond configuration.

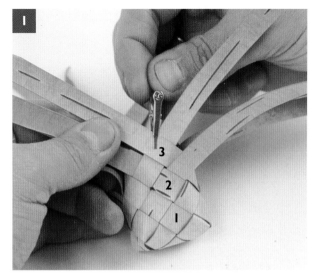

Turn the basket so that the outside is facing out. On the sides, weave up three diamonds.

Turn the basket to the other base corner (photo 7), and work the third and fourth corners exactly the same way (photo 8).

On one end, weave up four diamonds for the neck of the saltcellar.

3

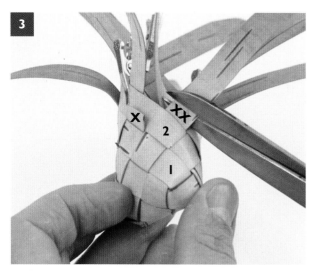

On the other end, weave up two diamonds. On the end that is two diamonds high, cut off two of the strips marked X and XX so that each cut end measures ¼ inch. This is the turn to the neck.

4

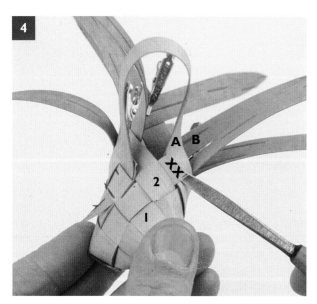

Thread strip A on the right (under the right cutoff end XX), and thread it on top of cutoff end X and under the next intersection.

5

6

Thread strip B, the next strip on the right (photo 5), on top of cutoff end XX (photo 6) and under the next intersection.

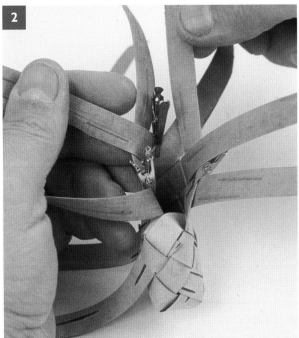

Pull the ends snug so that they form tight corners.

Saltcellar Neck

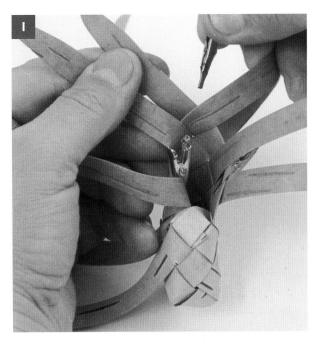

Take off the microclip on the back of the basket (photo 1), and release the last row on both the right and left sides (photo 2).

3

Put a microclip on the new intersection.

4

Hold the basket so that the "turn to the neck" is facing you.

5

Take the strips going from the turn to the neck.

6

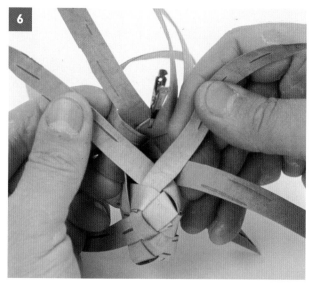

Start weaving the neck by weaving the right strip under the left.

7

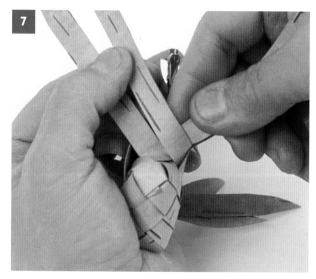

Weave the left strip under the next right strip.

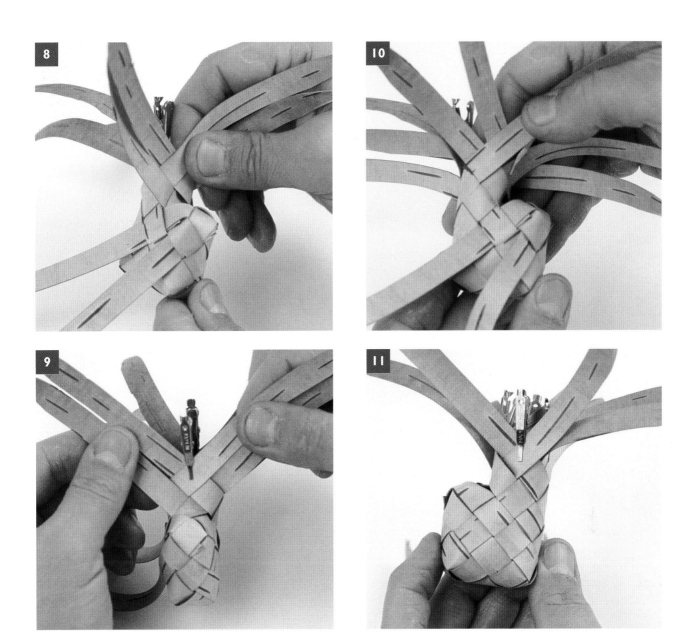

Photos 8–11: Working to the left, weave each of the strips for one row. Secure each step with a microclip.

Weave one more row all the way around so there are two diamonds above the turn to the neck and the left-pointing strips are on the outside.

Saltcellar Rim

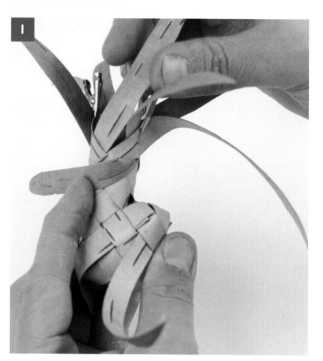

Unweave two strips. Fold the left-pointing strip down at a right angle (photo 1), and thread it under the first intersection on the side (photo 2).

3

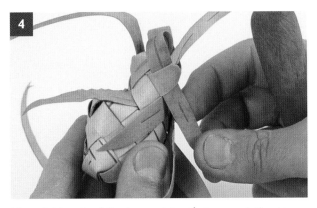

Working to the left, continue to work the rest of the rim the same way.

4

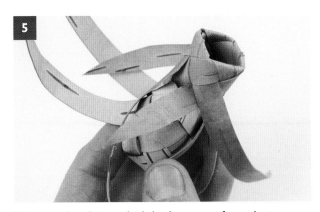

Next, fold each of the inner strips that are pointing to the right at a right angle, threading them under only the one layer that is formed by the first rim strips.

5

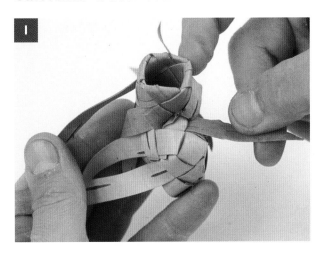

The completed rim, which looks square from the top.

Saltcellar Outer Wall

1

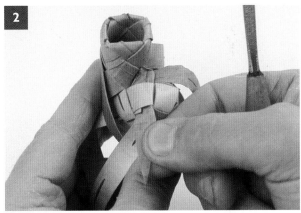

Thread each of the strips from the neck down the sides as far as they will go.

2

Cut off the strips used for the turn to the neck.

4

5

6

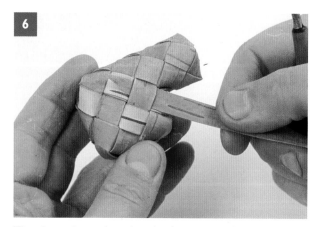

They have the underside side showing, so they can't be used to weave down the sides. Save them to use for covering the outside of the basket with the right sides out.

The completed saltcellar, before embellishment.

EMBELLISHMENT, THE PINWHEEL DESIGN

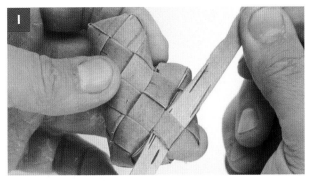

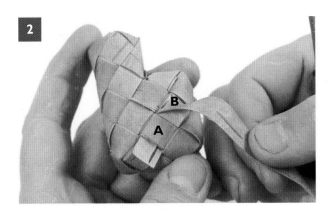

This pinwheel embellishment adds strength to the sides of the saltcellar. Work one on each side in a counter-clockwise direction. Add a new 8-inch strip, underside up, under diamond A on one side.

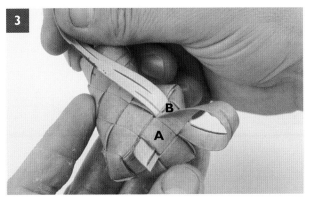

Fold it on a diagonal to the right (photo 2); then thread the end, underside up, through diamond B (photo 3). Press each fold flat.

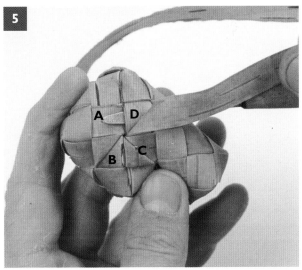

Continue this sequence for the next two sides of the pinwheel, folding and threading through diamond C (photo 4) and diamond D (photo 5).

6

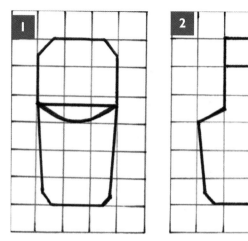

End by threading the strip up under diamond A on top of the beginning end.

7

Trim the ends.

The finished saltcellar with embellishment added.

WOODEN STOPPER

1

2

Carve the stopper from a 2 × ½ inch block of basswood (also called linden) or pine.

Carve the bottom inch of the stopper on a taper from ½ inch at the bottom to a scant ⅝ inch (or the size to fit the opening) at the widest point 1 inch up. Carve in about ⅛ inch on each side to form the top, which is approximately ¼ inch thick, as shown in the drawing (left) by Flo Hoppe. Cut the side points off at an angle. Also, chamfer the bottom edges where the stopper goes into the neck of the basket. The profile of the stopper is shown in the drawing (right) by Flo Hoppe.

project eight

Sawtooth-Rim Basket with Feet

Weaving Level
beginner to advanced

Dimensions
base of finished basket 4½ × 3½ inches;
height 2½ inches

Materials
½-inch birch-bark strips: 20 for the
basket, each 19 inches long; 16 for the
feet, each 6 inches long; and 20 for
the embellishment, each 4 inches long

Preparation
Rub vegetable oil on each of the strips.
Cut both ends of each of the twenty
19-inch strips to a rounded point. Cut
one end of each of the sixteen strips for
the feet to a rounded point. Cut one end
of each of the twenty 4-inch strips for
the embellishment to a rounded point.

*T*his basket is a contemporary style and popular with Vladimir's students. The basic basket is made with the usual diagonal plaiting. The sawtooth rim is different from a regular rim, but easy to make. The sides are embellished with a split-diamond design that echoes the sawtooth rim. The feet add another dimension to the basket.

The finished sawtooth-rim basket with feet.

135

WEAVING THE SAWTOOTH-RIM BASKET WITH FEET
Basket Base

The base consists of 10 vertical and 10 horizontal strips. Weave the base according to the general basket-making directions in chapter 6. (The horizontal strips in the example are lighter than the vertical strips, but they are all right side up.) Make sure the strips are close together with no holes, and secure the corners with microclips. The base weaving measures 4½ inches square. Make sure the base is absolutely square.

Basket Side Corners

The location of the side corners is the same as in project 5 (Oval Basket with Curls): between strips 4 and 5.

Working across the inside of the basket, weave three strips on each side of the corner space so that you have a 6-diamond configuration (photos 2 and 3). Do this with each of the other three corners (photo 4).

Basket Sides (Inner wall)

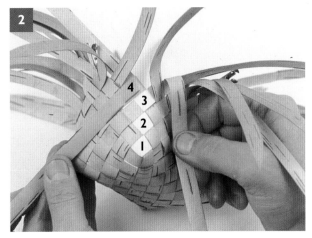

Weave on the outside of the basket to a height of four diamonds. Count the diamonds at a corner, making sure the basket is the same height all the way around. When the row is complete, all of the outer strips will be pointing left.

Fold strip 4 down on top of itself.

Sawtooth Rim

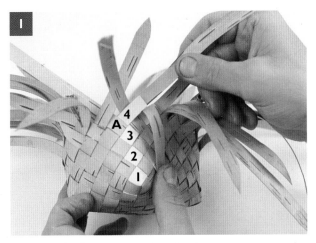

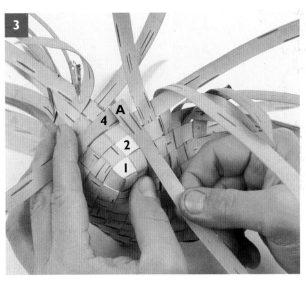

Unweave the last row in pairs of strips as you weave around the rim. Press each of the folds flat as you turn them down. Unweave two strips at the corner so that the fourth diamond strip is on top pointing to the right, as shown here.

Unweave the next two strips to the left and fold strip A across strip 4.

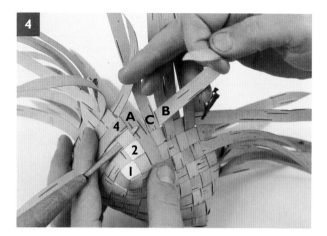

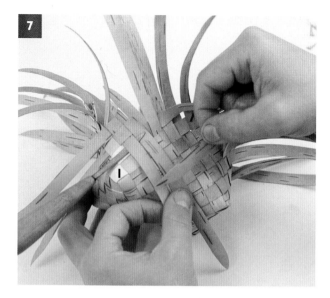

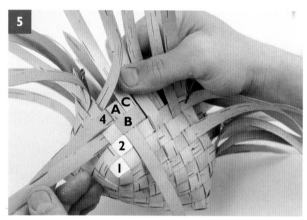

Working to the right, unweave strips B and C. Fold strip B down across strips C and A, and thread it under the first intersection.

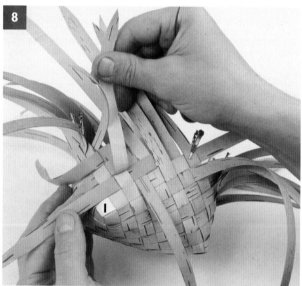

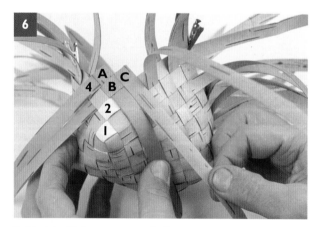

Fold strip C down over strip B.

Working to the right, continue this sequence of unweaving the next two strips, then folding the right-pointing strip down and threading it under the first intersection (as shown in the photos), and folding the left-pointing strip down on top of it. Do this for the entire rim.

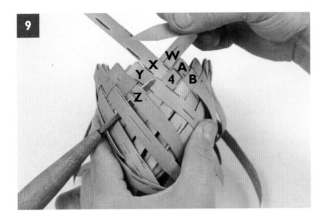

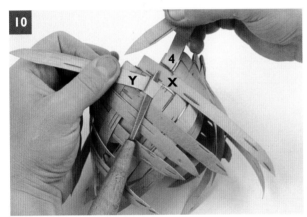

To end, bring strip W over strips X and Y and under the intersection underneath strip Z (photo 9). Lift up strip 4, and fold strip X down to the right (photo 10). Lift up strip Y, and thread strip 4 under the intersection (photo 11). Pull all the strips snug to make sure the edge is tight and even.

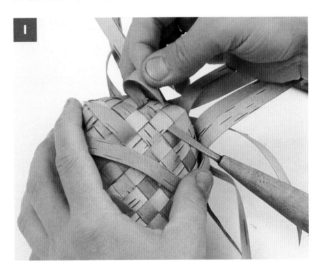

The completed sawtooth rim.

Basket Outer Wall

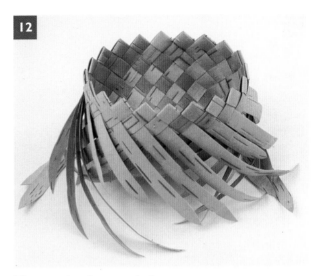

Thread each of the strips down the sides and across the bottom.

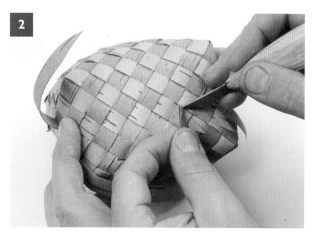

Trim the ends with a craft knife.

The finished basket with sawtooth rim.

Basket Feet

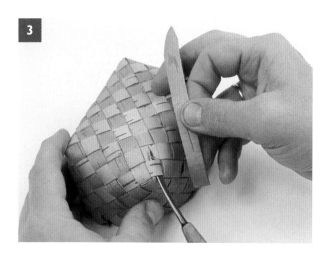

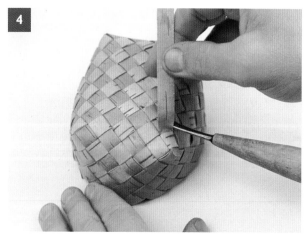

Add strips as necessary.

The feet are woven at each corner by threading four 6-inch strips through the marked diamonds. With the underside of the strips facing up, thread them from the top of the basket down, leaving ⅛ inch extending above the diamond. To begin, thread strip A under diamond No. 1 from the upper left to the lower right, as shown here.

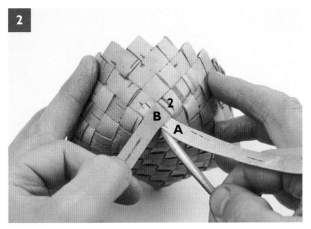

Thread strip B under diamond No. 2 from the upper right to the lower left.

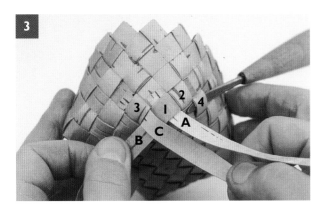

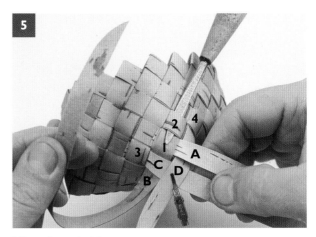

Microclip to hold.

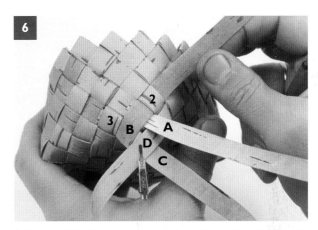

Fold strip B back on itself, and thread it under diamond 2.

Thread strip C under diamond No. 3 from the upper left to the lower right, and weave strip C over strip B. Thread strip D under diamond No. 4 from the upper right to the lower left, and weave strip D under strip A and over strip C (photo 4).

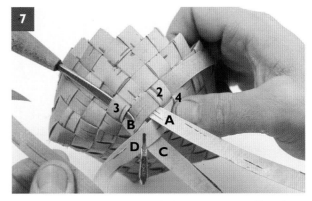

Fold strip D at a right angle. Weave it over strip B and under diamond 3, as shown here.

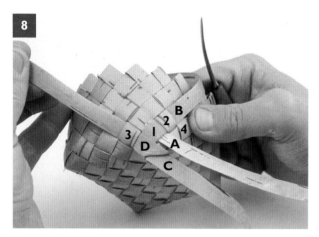

8

Press the fold flat.

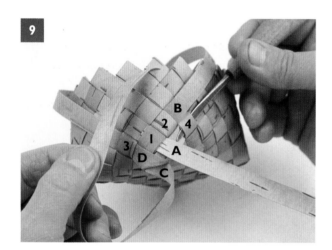

9

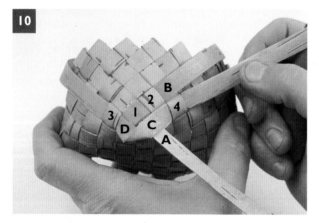

10

Fold strip C at a right angle. Bring it over strip A, and thread it under diamond 4, as shown here.

11

12

Fold strip A back on itself. Bring it over strip C, and thread it under diamond 1, as shown here.

13

Thread each of the strips under one more diamond, and then trim.

14

15

The finished foot.

EMBELLISHMENT, SPLIT DIAMONDS

1

Each of the split diamonds is woven with a separate strip. Thread a 4-inch strip under a weaver two diamonds down from the top between the peaks of the rim.

Thread the strip, underside up, from the lower right to the upper left, leaving ¼ inch extending below the diamond.

2

Fold the strip down to the left at a right angle.

3

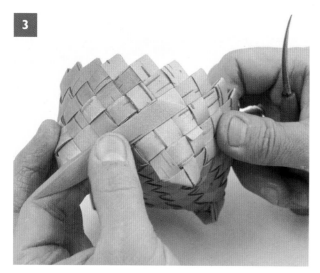

Press it flat across the lower half of the diamond.

4

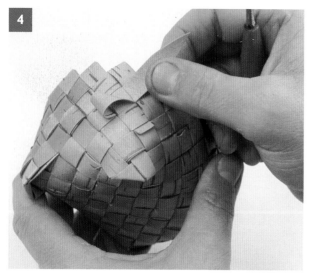

Release the fold as you thread the end under the diamond where you've made the fold from the lower left to the upper right.

5

The fold.

6

Fold the strip at a right angle up to the left and press it flat.

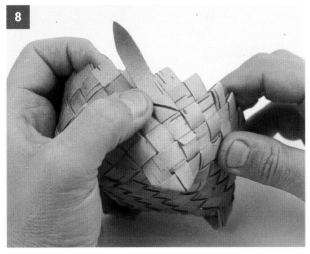

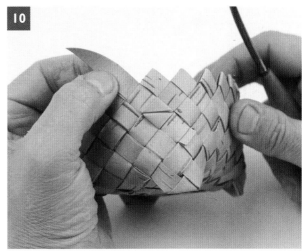

Fold it down across the top half of the diamond and press it flat.

Release the fold as you thread the end under the diamond on a diagonal up to the left, as shown in the photos. Work split diamonds in each of the remaining 19 diamonds around the side. Trim all the ends with a craft knife.

project nine

Peasant Basket with Handle

Weaving Level
beginner to advanced

Dimensions
base of finished basket 4¾ × 3¾ inches;
basket height 2⅝ inches; height with
handle 5 inches

Materials
26 birch-bark strips, ½ inch × at least
19 inches; 18 inches of narrow willow
rod or No. 5 round reed for a rim core

Preparation
Rub vegetable oil on each of the strips
with a small rag. Cut both ends of each of
20 strips for the basket to a rounded
point. Cut one end of each of three strips
for the three-part braid to a rounded
point. Cut both ends of each of three
strips for the handle to a rounded point.

*T*his peasant basket with a handle is very traditional in
Russia. The basket is made with the same diagonally
plaited techniques used for the oval basket with curls
(project 5), but the rim is reinforced with a piece of willow or
reed to make it stronger for the handle to be inserted. The braid
also adds strength to the rim. This basket can be made in many
different sizes and used for collecting berries and mushrooms or
vegetables grown in a kitchen garden.

The finished peasant
basket with handle.

WEAVING THE PEASANT BASKET

Peasant Basket Base

The base consists of 10 vertical and 10 horizontal strips. Work the base according to the general basket-making directions in chapter 6. Make sure the strips are close together with no holes, and secure the corners with microclips. The base weaving is 4½ inches square. Make sure the base is absolutely square.

Peasant Basket Side Corners

The location of the corners is the same as with the oval basket with curls—between strips 4 and 5. Work the corners as you did for that project.

Peasant Basket Sides (Inner Wall)

Weave the sides to five diamonds. Count the diamonds at the corner, making sure the basket is the same height all the way around. This is one more row woven for stability. The rim strips are all pointing to the right.

Peasant Basket Rim

Unweave the two strips at the corner so that you can turn down the strip pointing to the left (strip number 4) at a right angle over the rim core.

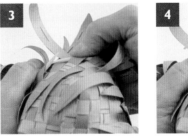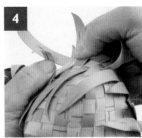

Scarf each of the ends of the rim core for ¾ inch. Scarf the outside of the beginning end and the inside of the final end so that the ends fit together smoothly.

Referring back to photo 1, place the rim core with the scarfed side out on the outside of the basket. Bring the left-pointing outer strip number 4 down over the rod at a right angle, and thread it under the first intersection.

Working to the right, continue to fold the outer strips in this manner for the first row of the rim (photo 2).

5

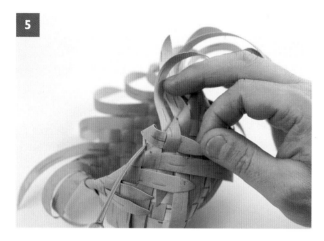

6

7

All the inner rim strips are pointing to the right. Working to the right, bring each strip, in turn, at a right angle and thread it under the one layer of the first rim row.

8

The last rim strip being threaded.

9

The completed rim.

Completing the Peasant Basket

I

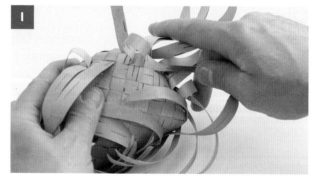

Thread each of the strips in one direction down to the middle of the bottom.

Thread the strips from the opposite direction, and overlap the ends on the bottom.

If you need to add a strip to make the double layer complete on all the strips, cut a short strip to a rounded point and thread it under the intersection where the strip is too short. Pull it all the way through, leaving 1/8 inch extending beyond the edge.

Weave the pointed end as far as it needs to go, and trim both ends of the added strip with a craft knife.

EMBELLISHMENT, THE BRAID

This is a continuous braid that begins and ends in the same place. It requires the strips to be worked three times around the basket to fill in all the spaces.

With the underside up, thread a strip under the top diamond marked with an X. Working to the left, fold the strip at a right angle and thread it under the next diamond. The right side of the strip appears on the upper part of the braid, and the underside on the lower part of the braid. Fold the strip up at a right angle, and thread it under the next top diamond.

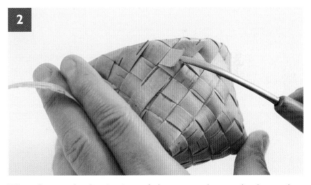

This shows the beginning of the second round where the strip goes under the diamond on which the beginning end is lying. Continue this sequence all the way around for three complete rounds. Add strips as necessary.

At the end, thread the final end under the beginning end.

The finished braid.

WEAVING THE HANDLE

If the birch bark for the handle is thick, two handle strips will be enough, with a third strip for wrapping the handle. If the bark is thin, three handle strips are better, with a fourth to wrap the handle.

The length of the handle from side to side when threaded onto the basket is half of the circumference of the top of the basket, or 7½ inches.

Cut the hole for the handle carefully with a knife. The horizontal cut is ½ inch wide and is made in the middle of the braid between two strips. This is very important!

Make the cut on half of one braid strip and half of the next braid strip so that nothing will unravel.

4

Thread the ends of a strip, right side up, through the holes in both sides of the basket from the outside to the inside.

5

Make the handle 7½ inches long, folding the extra inside length up against the underside of the handle. Thread a second strip through the holes the same way so that there are two strips together, as shown here. (Add a third strip if necessary.) Microclip the inside ends against the handle.

6

A third (or fourth) strip will wrap the other two (or three) handles together. Thread it from the outside to the inside, putting the short inside end up against the handle. Start wrapping to the right with the long end, as shown here.

7

8

Wrap once around, and then on the second wrap, go between the two handle strips (or underneath the upper handle strip) for the beginning of an over/under pattern.

Wrap in this over/under pattern, which appears only on the top, across the entire handle.

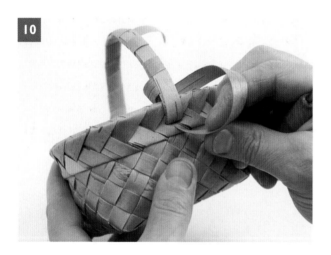

Thread the end from the outside to the inside (photo 10), and run it under the final inside wrap (photo 11). In photo 11, you can also see where a strip has been added at the top of the handle. Trim all these ends with a craft knife (photo 12).

project ten

Treasure Box with Lid

Weaving Level
intermediate to advanced

Dimensions
base of finished box 5 × 3¹/₂ inches;
height 4³/₄ inches

Materials
90 birch-bark strips, ¹/₂ inch × at least 19 inches

Preparation
1. Rub vegetable oil on each strip with a small rag.
2. Cut these birch-bark strips:
    • 20 for the basket, each 19 inches long—Cut both ends of each strip to a rounded point.
    • 20 for the lid, each 15 inches long—Cut both ends of each strip to a rounded point.
    • 40 for the flange on the basket, each 6 inches long—Cut one end of each strip to a rounded point.
    • 40 for the flange on the lid, each 6 inches long—Cut one end of each strip to a rounded point.
    • 4 for the knob on the lid, each 10 inches long—Cut one end of each strip to a rounded point.
3. Cut one long ¹/₂-inch-wide strip in half lengthwise to make two ¹/₄-inch-wide strips for the basket and lid embellishment. Cut one end of each strip to a rounded point.

*T*his project provides an opportunity to learn several interesting techniques. The basket and the lid are made the same, except for the height. A flange (or rim) is woven one-diamond down on the outside of the basket to provide a ledge for the lid to sit on. A flange is woven on the outside of the lid so that the lid goes over the basket ledge and the two fit perfectly together. The knob on the lid is woven in a crown knot pattern and topped with a pinwheel decoration. A diagonal curl embellishment finishes off both the basket and the lid.

The finished treasure box with lid.

The finished basket (left) and lid (right), without embellishment.

WEAVING THE TREASURE BOX
Treasure-Box Base
The base for the basket and the base for the lid each consist of 10 vertical and 10 horizontal strips. Weave the bases according to the general basket-making directions in chapter 6.

Treasure-Box Side Corners
The location of the side corners is the same as in project 5 (Oval Basket with Curls)—between strips 4 and 5 (see Side Corners, photo 1, page 109 in project 5).

Weave the corners as you did for the oval basket (see Side Corners, photos 4 and 5, page 110 in project 5).

Treasure-Box Sides (Inner Wall)
Weave on the outside of the basket to a height of five diamonds before working the rim. The finished basket will be four and a half diamonds high.

Weave on the outside of the lid to a height of two diamonds before working the rim. The finished lid will be one and a half diamonds high as shown in photo 1 (right) with the finished basket, without embellishment.

TREASURE-BOX RIMS
Weave the rims for the basket and the lid the same way. Weave the basket up to five diamonds high. The outer strips will all be pointing to the right. When the rim is finished, it will be four and a half diamonds high (see photo 1 below). Count the diamonds at the corners, and make sure the entire basket is even with the corner height all the way around. Fold the right-pointing strip (diamond number 4½) down at a right angle, and thread it under the first intersection, as in project 6, Bottle with Stopper Rim, photos 1 and 2 on pages 119 and 120. Working to the right, fold the right-pointing strip at a right angle, threading it under the first intersection (project 6, photo 3 on page 120). Work this way around the entire basket.

Now work the inner strips that are pointing to the left. Fold each of them down at a right angle, and thread them under only one layer—the layer formed by the first folded strip (project 6, photo 4 on page 120). After the rim is complete, pull each strip snug to make the edge of the rim tight and even.

Weave the lid to two diamonds high. When the rim is finished, it will be one and a half diamonds high, as shown in photo 1 below. Count the diamonds at the corners, and make sure the entire lid is even with the corner height all the way around. Work the lid rim the same way as the basket rim.

Basket and lid showing the number of diamonds high.

Basket Flange

The flange on the basket will create a one-diamond-row ledge at the top of the basket for the lid to fit over.

Forty strips are needed for the outside flange. After all 40 strips are threaded into the basket, the top edge of the flange is worked just like a rim. The ends are then threaded down to the bottom edge and cut off.

Begin by threading a 6-inch strip underside up, through the second diamond from the top edge (diamond 1). Thread it from the lower left to the upper right.

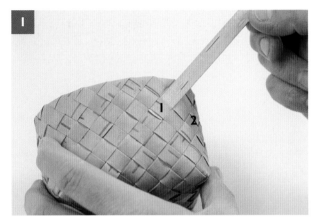

Go to the right and thread the second strip through diamond 2 from the lower right to the upper left. Weave it under the first strip.

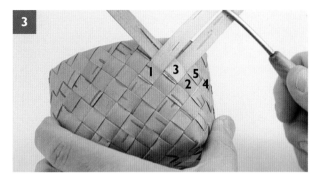

Go to the right and thread the third strip through diamond 3 from the lower left to the upper right.

Continue this sequence around the entire basket: Thread in a right-pointing strip and then a left-pointing strip which is woven under and over the last two right-pointing strips (photo 4).

Here is the completed rim with the outer strips pointing to the left.

For the rim, unweave two of the strips and fold the right-pointing strip down at a right angle.

Fold the left-pointing strip down at a right angle over the first strip.

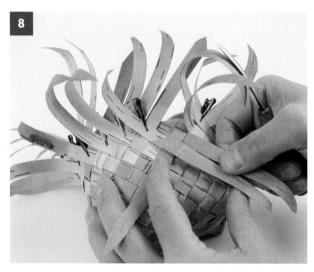

Working to the left, unweave the next two strips and fold the right-pointing strip at a right angle down over the last strip.

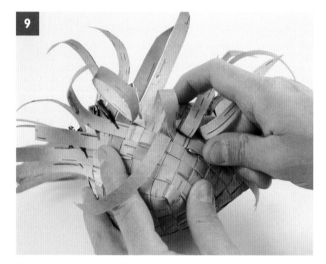

Thread it under the first intersection.

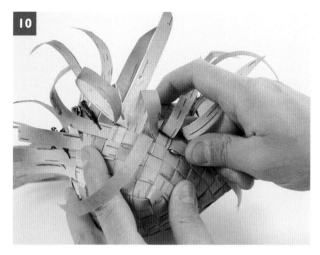

Continue working to the left, unweaving two strips, and folding down the left-pointing strip at a right angle to the left, and then the right-pointing strip at a right angle to the right (photo 10), and threading it under all layers of the side weaver (photo 11).

Finished flange border.

Thread all the ends down to the bottom edge of the basket, and then trim. Because the basket is already double-woven, the ends of the flange do not need to be threaded entirely across the bottom.

Finished basket with unfinished lid.

Lid Flange

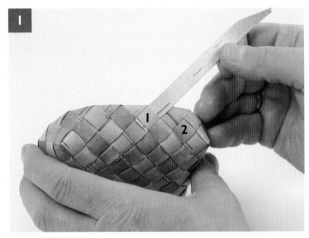

Thread the 40 strips for the lid flange as you did for the basket flange. The placement is higher, because the flange extends beyond the edge of the lid for one diamond, matching the height of the ledge on the basket.

Thread the first strip, underside up, through diamond 1, which is at the edge of the lid, as shown here.

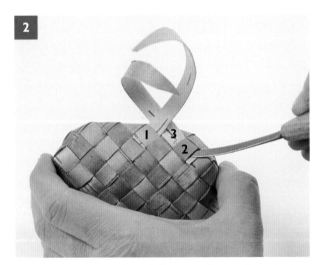

Go to the right and thread the second strip through diamond 2, and weave it under the first strip as shown here.

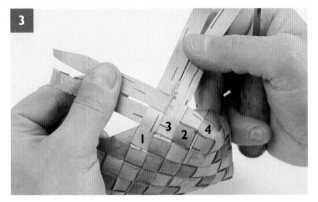

Weave the left-pointing strips under-one/over-one with the right-pointing strips.

The outer strips are all pointing to the left.

The lid flange rim is turned down at one diamond high as seen from the inside.

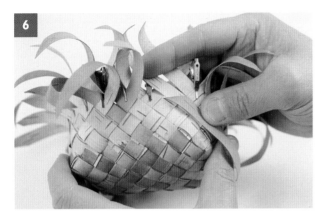

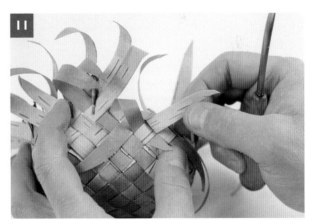

Work this rim the same as you did for the rim on the basket.

The completed flange rim from the inside of the lid.

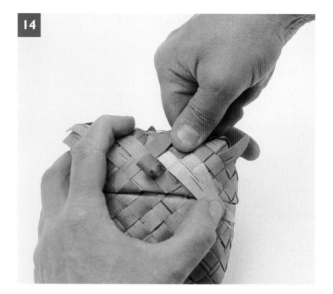

Make sure the lid fits on the basket. The lid rim can be adjusted by pulling on the ends to make the rim even all the way around.

Thread all the ends to the top edge of the lid, and then trim. The ends don't need to be threaded all the way across the top.

EMBELLISHMENT, EYEGLASS CURL

The diagonal curl on the sides of the basket and lid is called an "eyeglass curl." It is made with two ¼-inch strips.

On the basket, thread one end through the full diamond at the top of the flange with the underside of the strip up. Then curl the end around and thread it through the next full diamond with the underside of the strip facing up.

Pull the end of the strip snug and flatten the curl. Overlap the ends at the beginning, and trim the ends flush.

Work the same sequence around the entire basket and lid.

LID KNOB

The lid knob is a crown knot worked for six rows and topped with a pinwheel design. The size is graduated every two rows by cutting off ¹⁄₁₆ inch from the outer edge of each of the strips.

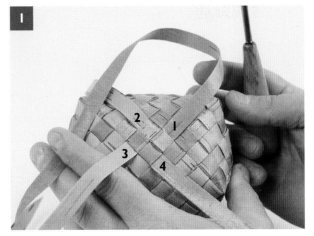

Take four 10-inch strips and thread them, right side up, through the top four diamonds, as shown in photo 1.

Rows 1, 3, and 5 of the crown knot are worked in a clockwise direction. Rows 2, 4, and 6 are worked in a counterclockwise direction.

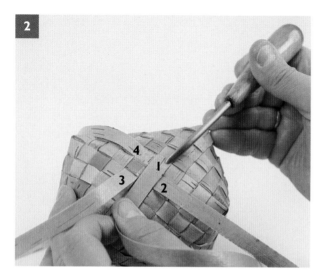

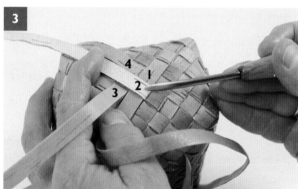

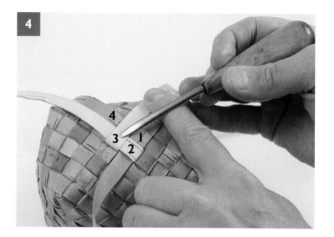

Row 1: Fold strip 1 back on itself (photo 2), strip 2 back on itself (photo 3), strip 3 back on itself (photo 4), and strip 4 back on itself, threading it through the loop formed by strip 1 (photo 5). The wrong side of the strips shows on this row.

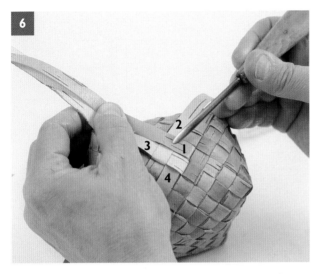

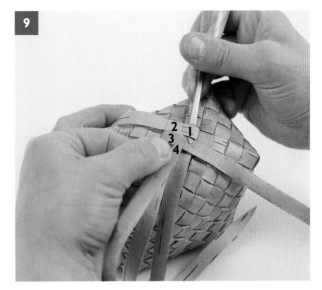

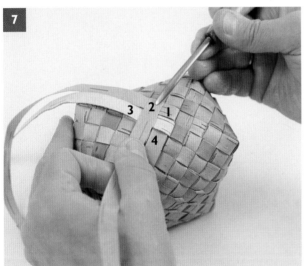

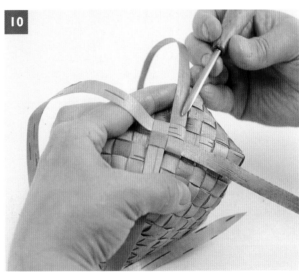

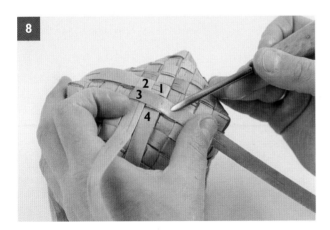

Row 2: Work in a counterclockwise direction. Fold strip 1 back on itself (photo 6), strip 2 back on itself (photo 7), strip 3 back on itself (photo 8), and strip 4 back on itself, threading it through the loop formed by strip 1 (photo 9). The right side of the strips shows on this row (photo 10).

Trim ¹⁄₁₆ inch off the left edge of each strip.

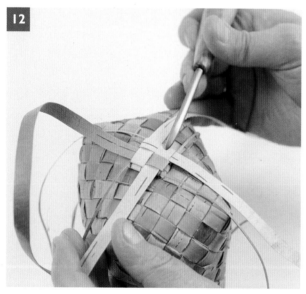

Work rows 1 and 2 again.

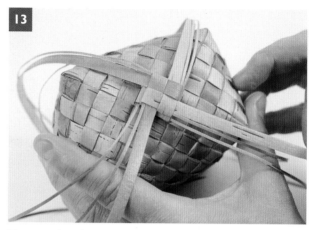

Trim another ¹⁄₁₆ inch off the left edge of each strip.

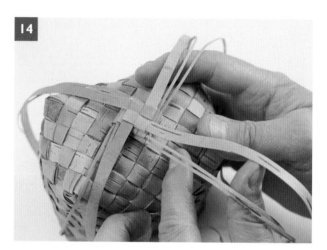

Work rows 1 and 2 again.

EMBELLISHMENT, PINWHEEL

The pinwheel is a continuous pattern worked with the same strip.

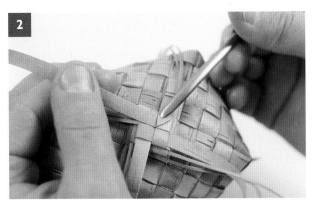

Fold one of the strips up at a right angle and press it flat.

Fold it in on top of the crown knot and again press it flat

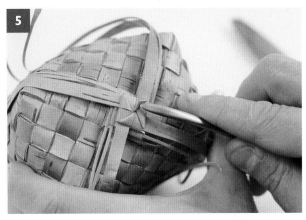

Thread the end under the adjacent weaver on the crown knot.

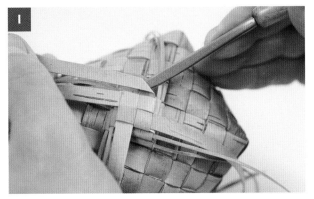

With the same strip, repeat this sequence two more times.

In order to thread the strip through the last strip on the crown knot, the first fold has to be cut.

Cut the fold with a craft knife on the outer edge (photo 4). Release the fold, creating a flap (photo 5).

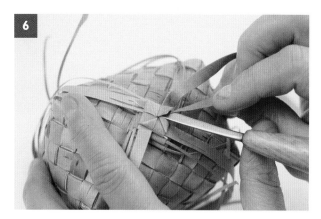

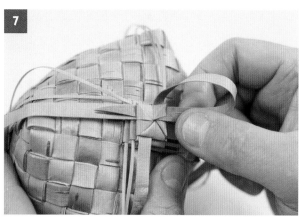

Thread the final end under the cut flap.

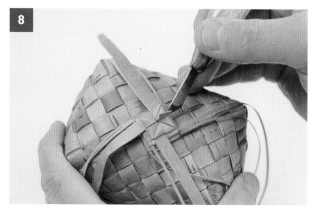

Trim off the flap.

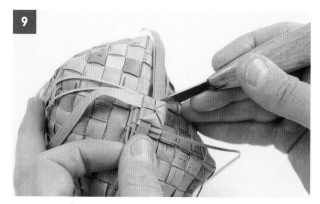

Trim all the strips on the outside edges of the crown knot.

Four related basket projects.

project eleven

Cube

Weaving Level
beginner to advanced

Dimensions
1-inch cube

Materials
two birch-bark strips, each ⅝ inch × 16 inches for the cube

Preparation
Cut one end of each strip to a rounded point.

Traditional birch-bark rattle, showing detail of handle, and birch-bark cubes in various sizes.

T*he cube is traditional in Russia and very old. Archeologists have found cubes in medieval sites in Novgorod. The peasants used them as rattles and, when made very large, as balls. The peasants in Russian villages used to play ball with cubes sewn with rags to make them stronger. The finished cube can be made into a rattle.*

In the gallery, the center photo on page 264 also shows how birch-bark cubes can be used as rattles with wooden handles.

WEAVING THE CUBE

The cube is made with two strips of birch bark that are
⅝ inch × 16 inches. With the underside up, fold each of
the two strips in the middle at a 90-degree angle.

Fold the right end around the back to the left.

Turn the strip over so that the right side is showing.

Place the right strip over the left strip so that it resembles an M.

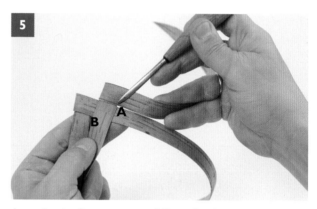

A marks the first corner and B marks the second corner.

Weave the right corner (A) first by bringing the right
strip under the next one to the left. Each time you weave,
you will be forming a corner, keeping all the strips tight.

Hold the three strips you've just woven firmly in place with your right hand.

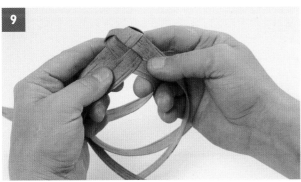

Make sure there are no holes between the strips. Weave the left corner (B) next by bringing the left strip over the next strip (photo 8) and under the following one (photo 9).

Make the same moves two more times, weaving first from the right and then from the left. Weave the right strip under one, and the left strip over one, under one. You will have created four sides of the cube at this point.

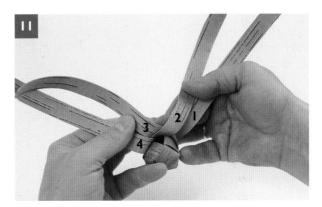

Flip the cube over from bottom to top, as shown here. There are two sets of strips, one set pointing to the right and one set to the left. Number them 1 to 4 from right to left.

Close the cube by threading the ends of the strips through the beginning part of the cube. These strips will make a complete second layer for the cube. For the best tension, use each of the weavers one move at a time, rather than threading one weaver at a time around the cube.

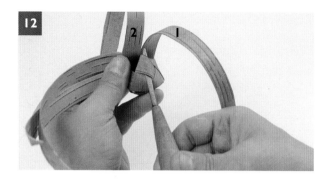

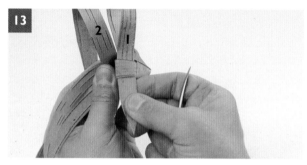

Take strip No. I and thread it under the beginning fold on the right.

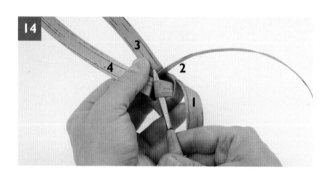

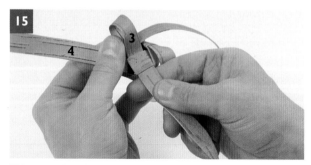

Take strip No. 3 and thread it under the beginning fold on the left.

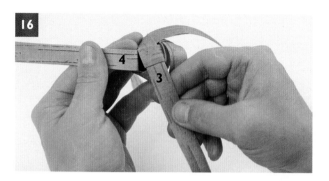

You can put seeds, rice, or popcorn in the cube at this point if you want to make a rattle.

Bring strip 4 over the beginning fold on the left, and thread it under the next intersection.

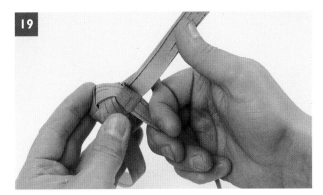

Pull the strip snug.

Bring strip 2 over the beginning fold on the right, and thread it under the next intersection.

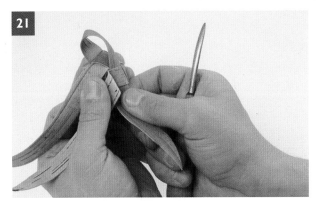

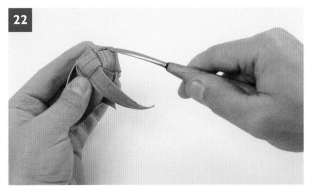

Continue to thread each of the strips in turn through the intersections of the cube, under all the layers, until you create a complete second layer.

Trim the ends.

The finished cube.

project twelve

Birch-Bark Bead Necklace

Weaving Level
beginner to advanced

Dimensions
32 to 33-inch necklace

Materials
two strips for the cube, ¼ inch × 10 inches; one strip for the four-sided bead, ½ inch × 8½ inches; 16 strips for the beads, ½ inch × 7½ inches; 16 strips for the beads, ⅜ inch × 7 inches; 30 strips for the beads, ⁵⁄₁₆ inch × 6½ inches; and 20 strips for the beads, ¼ inch × 6 inches.

Preparation
Rub vegetable oil on each strip with a small rag. Cut one end of each strip into a rounded point.

*C*ontemporary basket makers in Russia like to design and make necklaces from birch bark. This necklace is made with one cube and 82 triangular beads in graduated sizes. All the beads are threaded on a sturdy string through the holes in the tips of the beads. The cube can be strung through the holes in the sides or the holes in the corners. The four-sided bead can be used instead of the cube in the middle of the necklace.

See the gallery on page 270 for other examples of birch-bark necklaces.

Finished necklace made with birch-bark beads. Also shown are three loose beads.

WEAVING THE TRIANGULAR BEAD

For the triangular bead, use one strip of birch bark that is $\frac{1}{2}$ inch × $7\frac{1}{2}$ inches. To form the bead, the strip is tied in a knot.

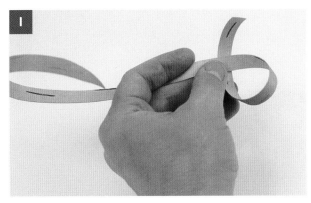

Hold the underside of the strip facing up with the pointed end to the left.

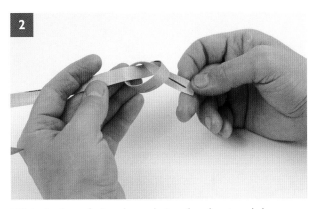

With the loop facing down, bring the short end down through the loop. Make sure you keep the underside up on the end you just pulled through, as shown here. This is very important.

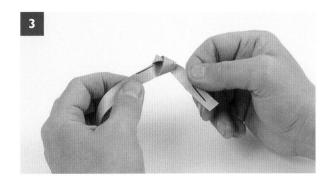

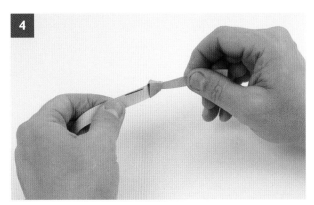

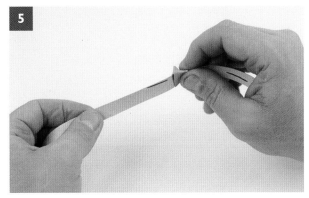

Pull the knot snug (photos 3 and 4), and pinch it with your right hand to form a triangular shape (photo 5).

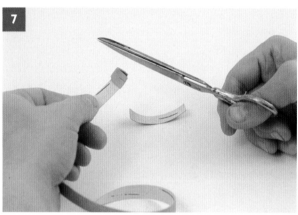

Trim the short end.

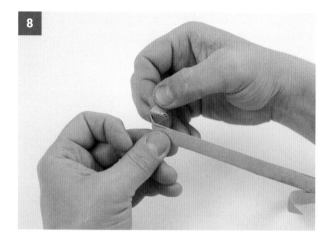

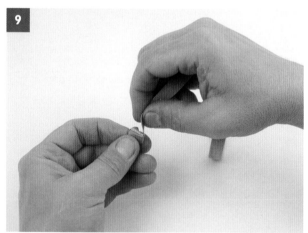

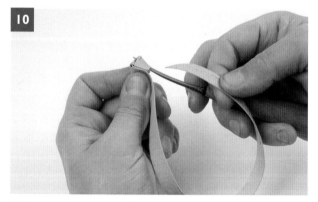

Wrap the long end around the bead for three sides (photos 8 and 9), and then thread the pointed end through the fourth side (photo 10).

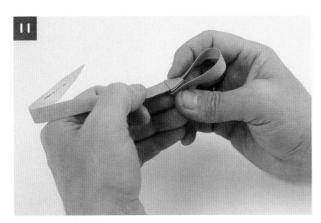

Pull the strip through and pull tight.

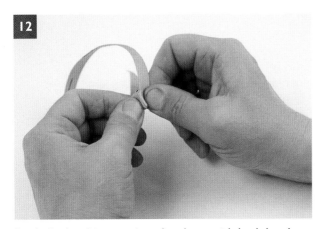

Pinch the bead into a triangular shape with both hands.

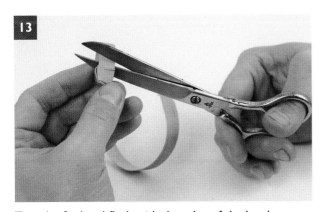

Trim the final end flush with the edge of the bead.

WEAVING THE FOUR-SIDED BEAD

Even though this bead is not used in the necklace, it is good to learn how to make it. This bead can replace the cube in the middle of the necklace.

Use one strip of birch bark that is $\frac{1}{2}$ inch $\times$ $8\frac{1}{2}$ inches. To form the bead, the strip is again tied in a knot.

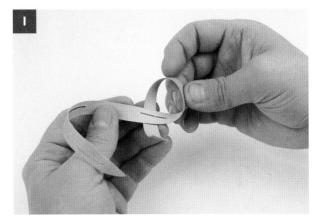

Hold the underside of the strip facing up with the pointed end to the left.

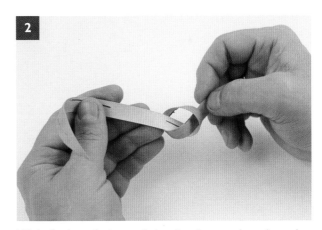

With the loop facing up, bring the short end up through the loop.

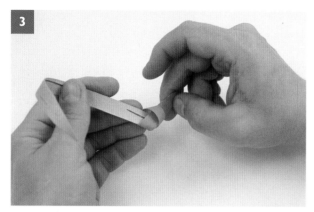

Make sure you turn the end you just pulled through so that the right side is facing out. This is very important.

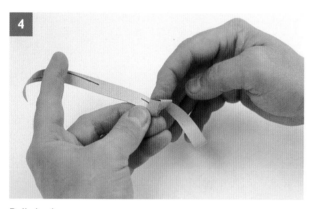

Pull the knot snug.

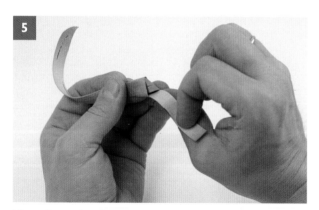

The other side of the bead. Notice that one end has the right side facing out and the other end has the underside facing out.

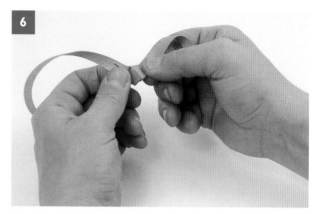

Form the four-sided bead with your fingers.

Trim the short end.

Wrap the long end around the bead for five sides.

Thread the pointed end through the sixth side.

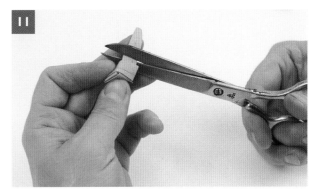

Pull the strip snug, and then trim off the end with scissors flush with the edge. And you're done.

The finished triangular bead (shown left) and the finished four-sided bead (shown right).

project thirteen

Offset Cube

Weaving Level
intermediate to advanced

Dimensions
1 1/2-inch cube

Materials
16 birch-bark strips, 1/2 inch × 14 inches

Preparation
Rub vegetable oil on each strip with a small rag. Cut both ends of each of eight strips to a rounded point. Cut one end of each of eight strips to a rounded point.

The offset cube is a contemporary design. It's a change from the regular symmetrical cube and offers a challenge in terms of shaping. This project throws out all the rules about where to turn the corners! If you pour some seeds into the cube, you can create a good toy for a child or a nice rattle for a friend.

The finished offset cube.

WEAVING THE OFFSET CUBE
Offset-Cube Base

Weave a 4 × 4 base with the right side of the strips up.

Offset-Cube Corners

1

Starting in the upper left corner, and going around in a clockwise direction, mark the corners between strips 1 and 2 (as shown in the Offset-Cube Base photo above). Weave each corner by taking the right weaver over the left (Offset-Cube Corners, photo 1). Secure the corners with microclips. The side weaving spirals up on an angle up to the left.

2

3

Row 1: With each left-hand-corner strip on each of the four sides, weave over one, under one, over one (photo 2). Secure with microclips (photo 3).

Row 2: With each left-hand-corner strip on each of the four sides, weave under one, over one, under one.

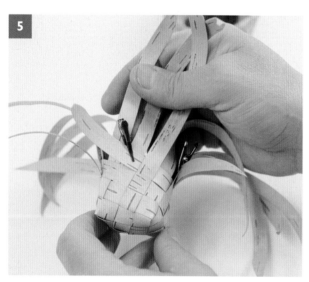

Row 3: With each left-hand-corner strip on each of the four sides, weave over one, under one, over one.

Offset-Cube Upper Corners

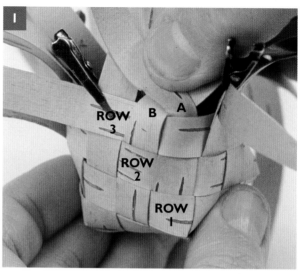

Weave a corner with the two strips above the third row by bringing strip A over strip B. Weave each of the other three corners the same way.

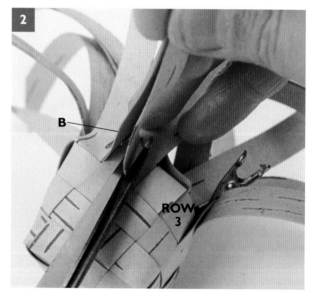

Turn the cube to the left so that the next surface to the right is facing you. There are two strips facing each other—strip B from the left and the row 3 strip on the right. Cut the right strip so that it lies in the middle of the over-weave, as shown here.

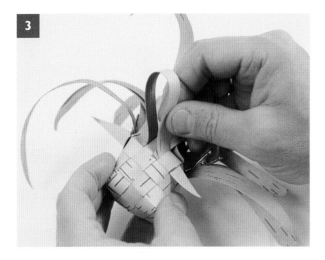

Thread strip B on top of the cutoff strip.

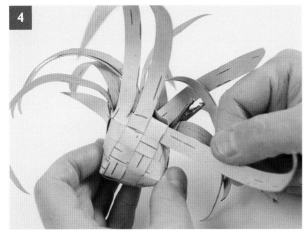

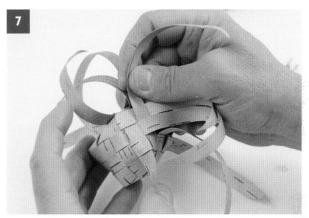

On the top of the cube, weave the first strip from the right under the next strip (photo 6) and over the following strip (photo 7).

Work the other three corners the same way. At this point, you can fill the cube with beans or rice if desired.

Cut the right strip off in the middle of the over-weave.

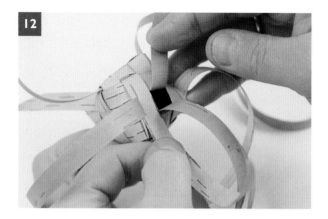

Lay the strip from the left on top of the cutoff strip (photo 9), and then thread it under one more intersection (photo 10).

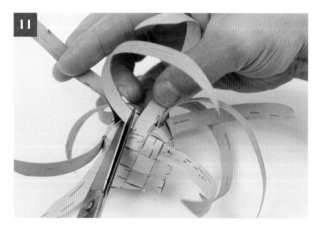

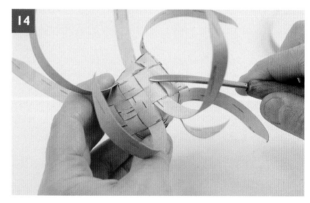

Do the same with the last four strips. Pull all the strips snug, so there are no holes between them. Cut off all the strips at this point (photo 14).

Weave the next strip from the right over, under, over, and cut it on top of the last over-weave, as shown here. Thread it under one more intersection.

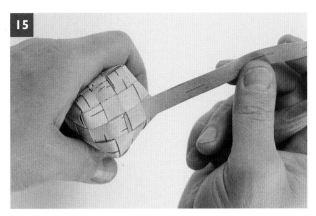

Thread the eight additional strips around the cube with the right side of the strips up until the entire cube has a second layer. Add more strips if necessary. Trim all the ends with a craft knife.

Various cubes with small kostyk.

project fourteen

Symmetrical Shoes

Weaving Level
advanced

Dimensions
base 5 × 2 inches; height 2 inches

Materials
24 birch-bark strips, ½ inch × at least 19 inches

Preparation
Rub vegetable oil on each of the strips with a small rag. Cut both ends of each of the strips to a rounded point.

Symmetrical shoes like these were made as long ago as the sixteenth century in northwest Russia. They are the traditional style mostly for women who used to wear them for farm duties such as feeding the cattle or milking the cow. Peasants also wore these shoes when mowing hay or harvesting berries and mushrooms in the forest. Today many customers want weavers to create these shoes for them because they remember seeing their parents or grandparents wear them. There are also requests to create tiny versions for small traditional cloth dolls.

Today, in Velikiy Novgorod, this type of shoe is popular as a souvenir. However, many people order these shoes from the masters not only in miniature but also in a wearable size. The Russian people take pride in the old handwork techniques that preserve traditional forms and methods, not allowing them to become a thing of the past but finding for them a place in contemporary industrial society.

WEAVING SYMMETRICAL SHOES
Shoe Base

These instructions are for weaving the left shoe. If you want to weave the right shoe, look at the pictures in a mirror to transpose the shaping.

For the left shoe, weave a 4 × 4 base, starting with the horizontal strip over the vertical strip in the lower left corner. Weave with the right side of the strips facing up. Secure the corners with microclips.

For the right shoe, weave a 4 × 4 base, starting with the vertical strip over the horizontal strip in the lower left corner.

Toe of Shoe

To form the toe on the left shoe, fold the two corner strips diagonally down across the center of the corner diamond.

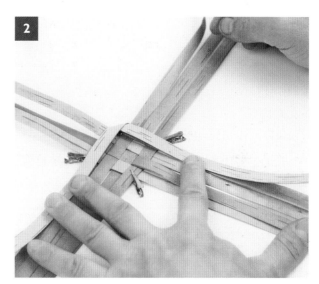

The left strip is over the right, and the corner is at a diagonal.

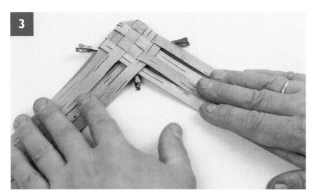

Weave the other three strips from each side into a 4 × 4 square identical to the first base. This is the sole, or underside, of the shoe.

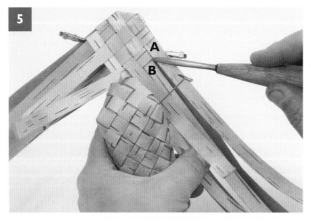

Mark the left corner between strips A and B on the left (photo 4) and strips A and B on the right (photo 5).

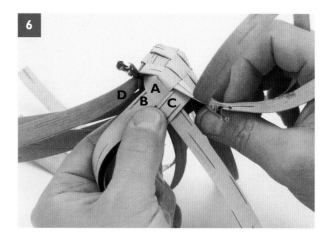

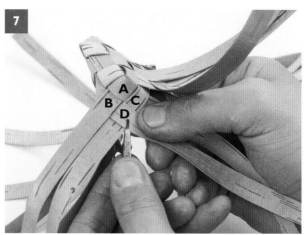

To form the left corner, weave strip A over strip B and under strip C (photo 6). Weave strip D under strip B and over strip C (photo 7).

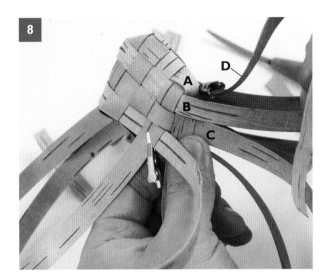

8

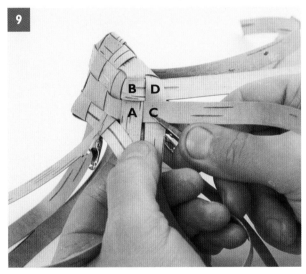

9

To form the corner on the right side of the toe, weave strip A under strip B and over strip C (photo 8). Weave strip D over strip B and under strip C (photo 9). Secure the corner with a microclip (photo 9).

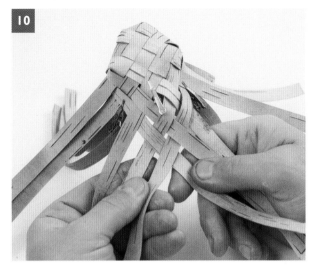

10

Weave all the strips coming from the corners on the left and the right into the middle of the sole.

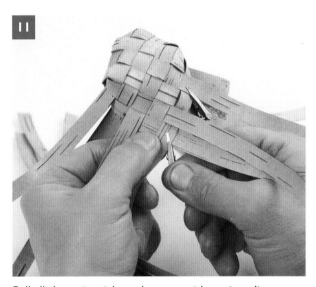

11

Pull all the strips tight and secure with a microclip.

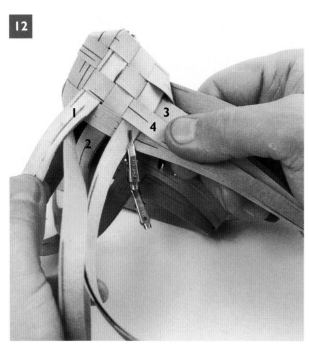

12

Turn the shoe over so that the top of the shoe is up. There are three strips on each side of the center. Three are facing to the left, and three to the right. The center two strips that are crossing and held by the microclip will not be woven at this point.

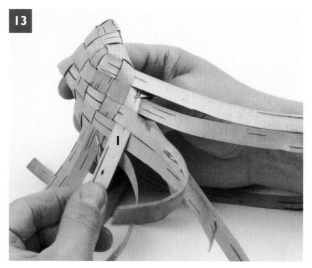

13

Take strip 1 from the top of the shoe on the left, and weave it as far as it will go on the underside.

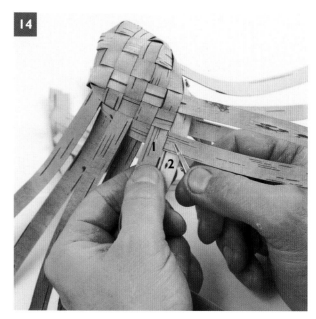

14

Take strip 2 from the top of the shoe on the left, and weave it as far as it will go on the underside.

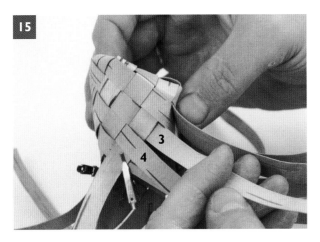

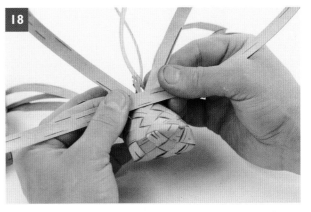

Place another strip, underside facing out, across the front of the crossed strips.

Take strips 3 and 4 (photo 15) from the top of the shoe on the right, and weave them, in turn, as far as they will go on the underside (photo 16).

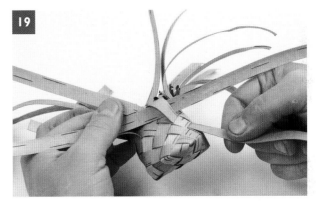

Bring the right strip over the new strip, and thread it under the first intersection on the right.

Turn the shoe over so that the top is up again. You will be working with the two strips that are crossed and held with the microclip.

Bring the left strip over the new strip, and thread it under the first intersection on the left.

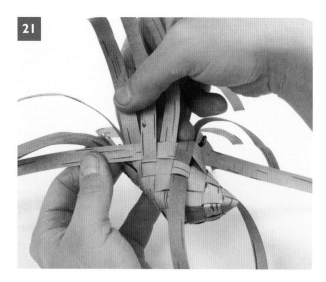

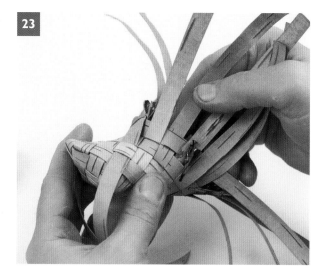

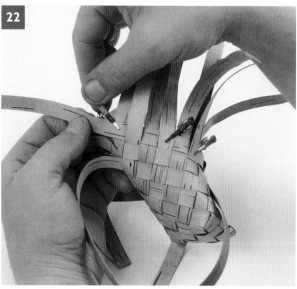

Weave the left end of the new strip to the left as far underneath as it will go.

Weave the right end of the new strip to the right (photo 23) as far underneath as it will go (photo 24).

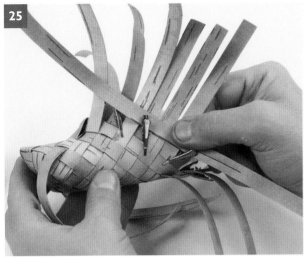

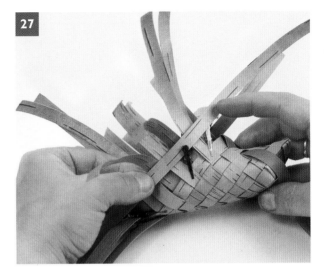

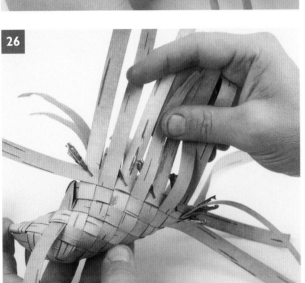

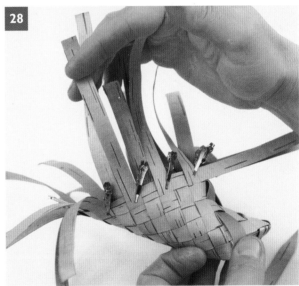

Place another strip, underside out, on the right side with one-third of the length above the shoe. Weave it as far underneath as it will go.

Place a second strip, underside out, on the left side with one-third above the shoe. Weave it as far underneath as it will go. These two added strips lengthen the shoe to make it in proportion to the shape of the foot.

Heel of Shoe

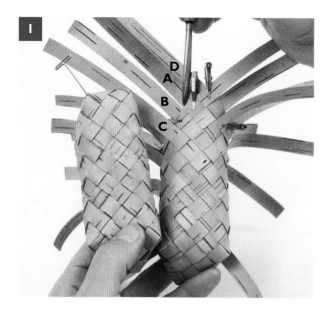

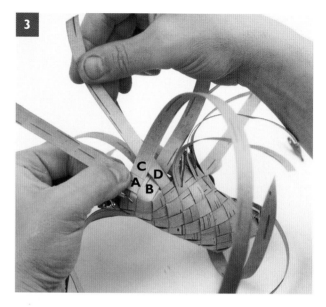

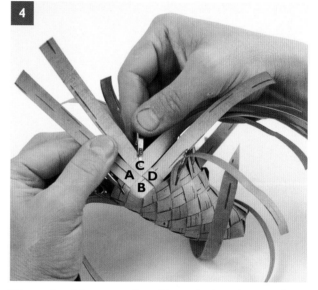

On the underside of the shoe, mark the heel corners between strips A and B on the left (photo 1) and strips A and B on the right (photo 2).

Weave the right corner by taking strip A under strip B and over strip C. Take strip D over strip B and under strip C (photo 3). This makes a four-diamond configuration; secure this with a microclip (photo 4).

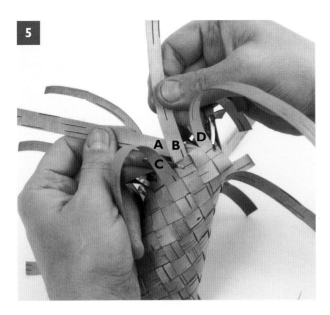

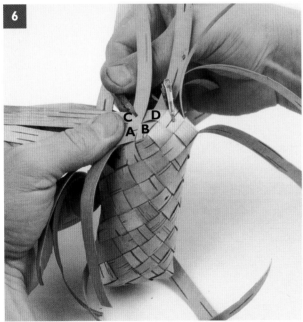

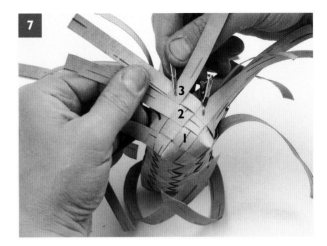

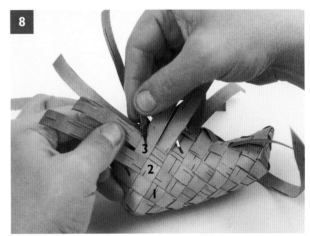

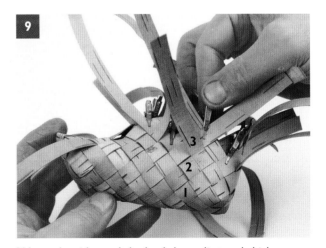

Weave the left corner the same way: Weave strip A under strip B (photo 5) and then over strip C (photo 6). Take strip D over strip B and under strip C (photo 6), and secure the four-diamond configuration with a microclip.

Weave the sides and the heel three diamonds high.

On the left side, bring the right strip over the inner rim only.

In the front of the shoe again, take an additional strip, and weave it over the right-angled strip and under the left-angled strip, centering it so there are equal lengths on each side. The two strips to the left and the two strips to the right of the crossed front strips will be woven over this strip just like with the plain-weave rim.

On the left side, bring the left strip over the outer rim, and then thread it under the next intersection.

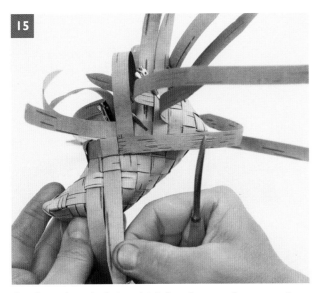

15

On the right side, bring the left strip over the outer rim, and then thread it under the next intersection.

16

On the right side, bring the right strip over the inner rim only.

Rim of Shoe

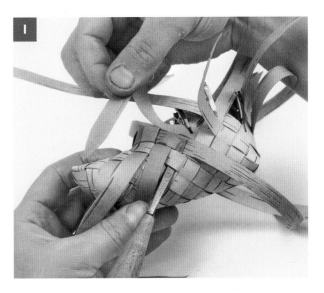

1

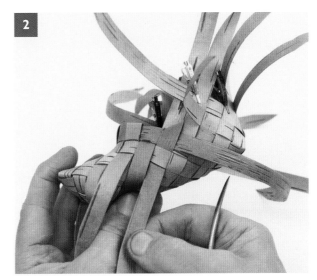

2

The next strip to the right is pointing up to the left. Fold this strip at a right angle over the added strip, and thread it under the next intersection.

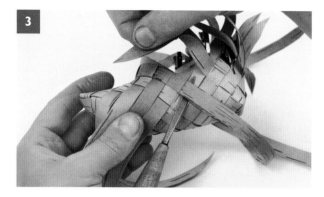

Unweave the next two strips to the right, and fold the left-pointing strip down at a right angle. Thread it under the next intersection.

Continue working to the right, unweaving the next two strips, and then folding each left-pointing strip down at a right angle and threading it under the next intersection. Work the rim this way around to the added strip on the other side, as shown here.

Lift up the added strip, and fold the right-pointing strip from the inside at a right angle.

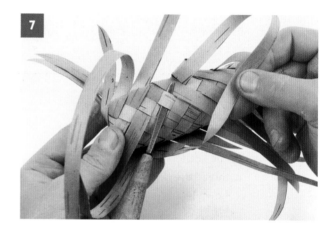

Bring the added strip over the folded strip, and thread it under the next intersection.

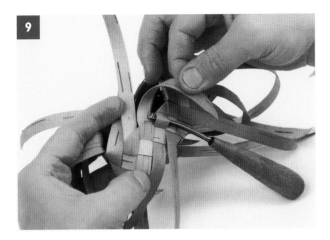

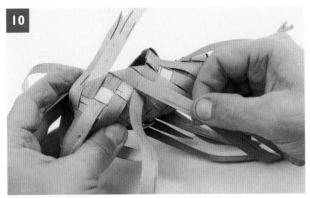

Working back to the left, fold each of the inside strips at a right angle and thread them under only one layer of the top diamond, as shown here.

The last rim strip on the right side.

The finished rim.

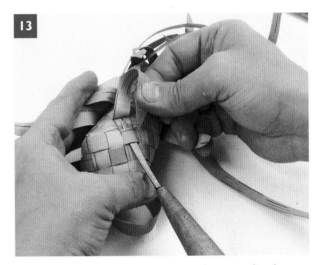

Thread each of the ends to completely cover the shoe with a second layer.

To weave the right shoe, look at the pictures in a mirror to transpose the shaping.

project fifteen

Fitted (Asymmetrical) Shoes

Weaving Level
advanced

Dimensions
base 5¼ × 2 inches; height 2 inches

Materials
24 birch-bark strips, ½ inch × at
least 19 inches

Preparation
Rub vegetable oil on each of the strips
with a small rag. Cut both ends of each of
the strips to a rounded point.

These fitted (asymmetrical) shoes have many similarities with the symmetrical birch-bark shoes from Project 14. The differences are in the initial layout and where the corners are turned for the toe. The techniques for the rest of the shoes are almost the same.

Finished pair of left and right asymmetrical
"fitted" birch-bark shoes.

WEAVING FITTED SHOES
Fitted-Shoe Base

For the left shoe, weave a 3 × 5 base, starting with the horizontal strip over the vertical strip in the lower left corner. Weave with the right side of the strips facing up. Secure the corner with microclips. In this photo, the awl points to the turning point for the left toe, the upper right corner of the base.

The base weaving for the right shoe is the same. The awl points to the turning point for the right toe, the upper left corner of the base.

Toe of Fitted Shoe

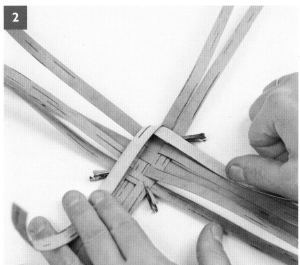

To form the toe on the left shoe, take the microclip off of the upper right corner (photo 1), and fold the two corner strips diagonally down across the center of the corner diamond (photo 2).

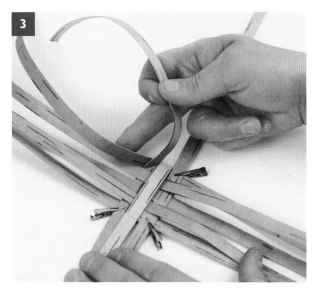

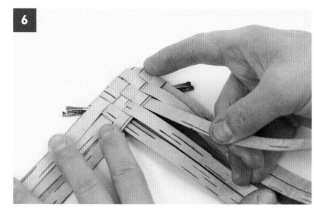

Interweave the three strips from the right with the five strips from the left so that you have a rectangular base identical to the first base.

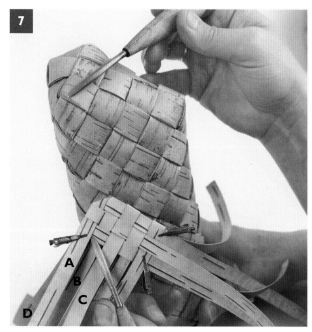

Turn the base over. The awl points to the place where the left corner is turned. Mark the left corner between strips A and B.

8

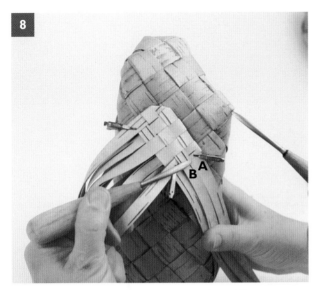

Mark the right corner between strips A and B.

9

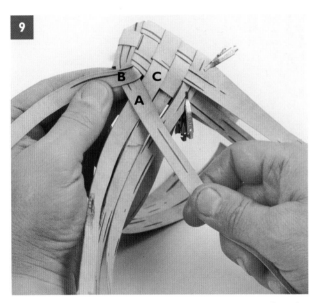

To form the left corner, weave strip A under strip B and over strip C.

10

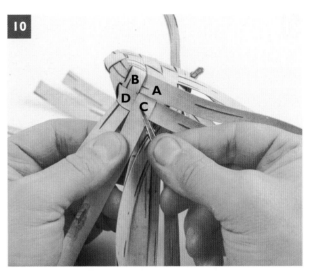

Weave strip D over strip B and under strip C. This forms a four-diamond configuration. Microclip the corner.

11

To form the right corner, weave strip A over strip B and under strip C.

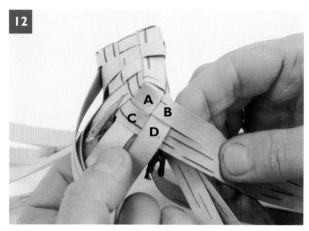

Weave strip D under strip B and over strip C to form a four-diamond configuration. Microclip the corner.

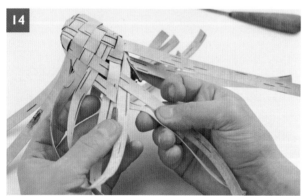

Weave the ends from each of the corners (photo 13) as far as they will go into the center of the underside (photo 14).

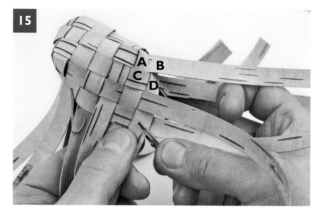

Pull them all tight and secure with a microclip.

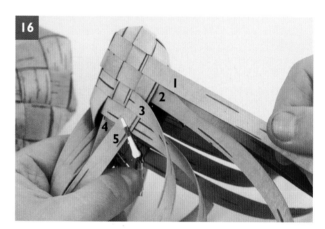

Turn the shoe over so that the top of the shoe is facing up. The strips are numbered 1 through 5.

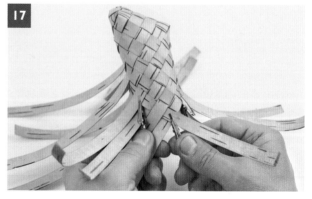

Weave them, in numerical order, as far as they will go on the underside. Pull them all snug. Secure with a microclip.

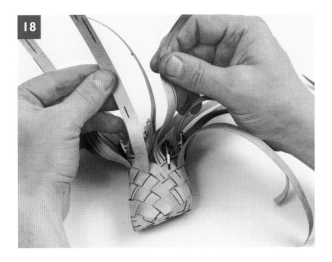

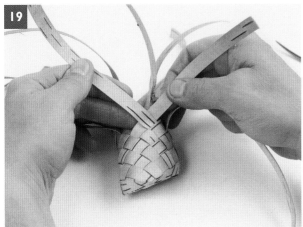

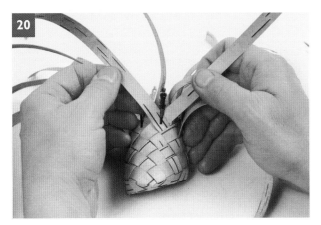

With the top of the shoe up, take the two center strips and cross the right strip over the left. Secure with a microclip.

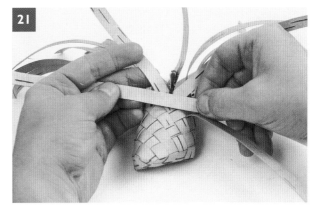

Take an additional strip and center it in front of the crossed strips, underside facing out.

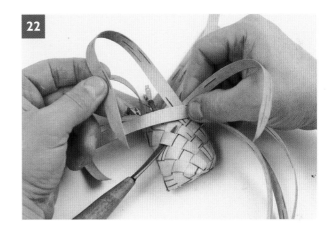

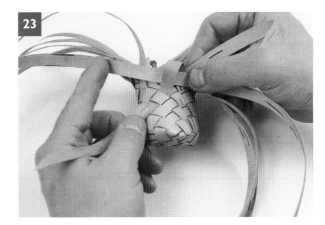

Bring the strip that is pointing up to the left over the added strip and under the first intersection.

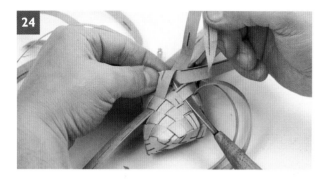

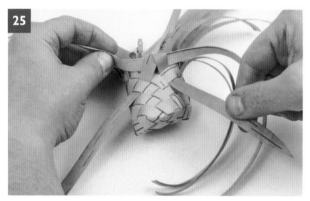

Bring the strip that is pointing up to the right over the added strip and under the first intersection.

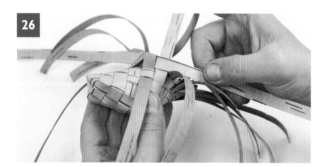

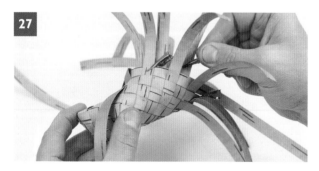

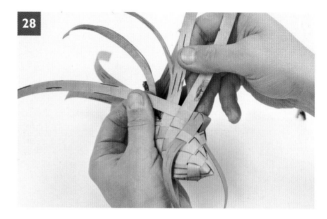

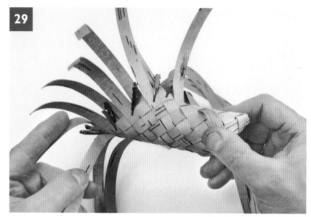

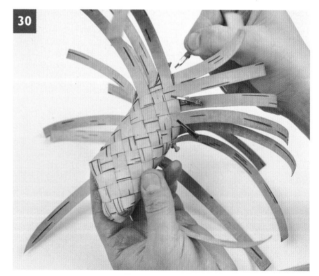

Weave the end of this additional strip on the right (photos 26 and 27) and on the left (photos 28 and 29) into the middle of the underside (photo 30).

Heel and Rim of Fitted Shoe

Take another strip, underside facing out, with one-third of the length above the shoe. Weave it from the right front (photo 31) to the middle of the underside (photo 32).

Turn the shoe over so that the underside is facing up. From this point on, the weaving of the heel corners and the rim is the same as for the symmetrical shoe, project 14 (the steps start with photo 1 on page 192).

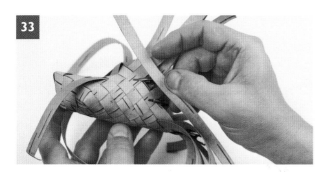

Do the same on the other side.

The finished left asymmetrical "fitted" shoe.

project sixteen

Canister

Weaving Level
advanced

Dimensions
base diameter 5 inches; height 7 inches

Materials
• Birch-bark cylinder, at least 1 mm thick.
• Sheet of birch bark, the same width as the cylinder plus a 6-inch overlap. It is 19 to 20 inches for this particular pattern.
• Three strips of birch bark for the vertical elements on the cylinder, each approximately 7 × 2½ inches.
• Birch bark rim strips: upper rim, 1¾ × 22 inches; lower rim, 2¼ × 22 inches.
• Unsplit spruce root, 3 mm thick × 11½ feet long.
• Bottom and lid, any conifer wood: pine, cedar, spruce. The diameter of the bottom and lid should be a little wider than the diameter of the cylinder. The thickness of the wood for the bottom is 1 cm and for the lid is 2 cm.
• Handle—willow, bird cherry, or mountain ash twig, 18 to 20 mm thick × 11½ to 12 inches long. We have used willow successfully; Russian peasants mostly used bird cherry.
• Handle wedge (the same wood as the handle), 2½ inches × 1 inch.

*S*olid-sheet birch-bark canisters (called tuesi) have been made in the city of Novgorod at least since the tenth century. Peasants used them to keep milk, sour cream, and honey fresh. Water and salt cucumber were stored in them as well. These canisters have been regarded as the highest form of birch-bark crafts. Creating the traditional canister with a single sheet inside the cylinder is a challenge, but after you have learned to shape the cylinder properly, you may consider yourself a master basket maker. The diameter of the cylinder is dependent on the tree from which it is harvested, so the measurement can vary. The instructions here are for a cylinder 5 inches in diameter.

Two views of the finished birch-bark canister.

WEAVING THE CANISTER

The inside of the canister is a seamless cylinder of birch bark. The outside of the canister is covered with a rectangular piece of birch bark 6 inches longer than the circumference of the inside cylinder.

Three rectangles decorate the outside of the canister. One is functional and two are decorative. They measure approximately 2½ × 7 inches. One of the rectangles covers the overlap on the outside (photo 2).

The other two rectangles are added to the outside, each one-third of the way around, to make a symmetrical design (photo 3).

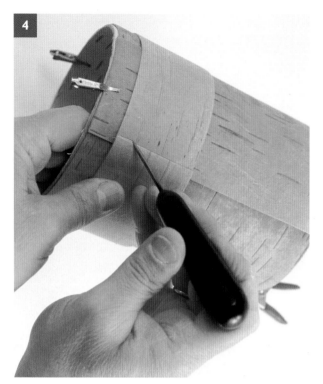

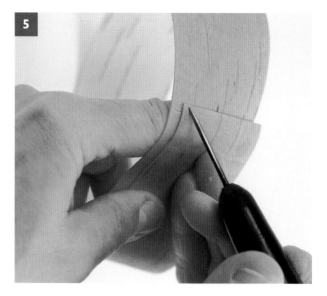

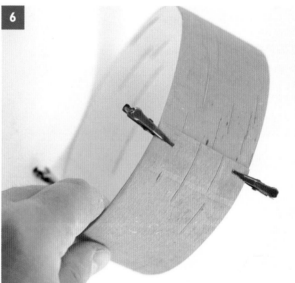

Two more strips are needed around the circumference as collars at the top and the bottom of the canister. The bottom collar measures 2¼ inches wide by the length of the circumference plus 6 inches. The 6-inch overlap is used to make the dovetail. The top collar measures slightly narrower (1¾ inches) to make the canister more visually balanced.

   Put the bottom collar on the canister as tightly as possible. Make a mark along the edge of the overlap.

Move the edge 4 to 5 mm past the mark and make another mark (photo 5). This new mark will ensure that the collar fits very securely. Microclip the collar at the top and the bottom on the second mark (photo 6). Do the same with the narrower top collar.

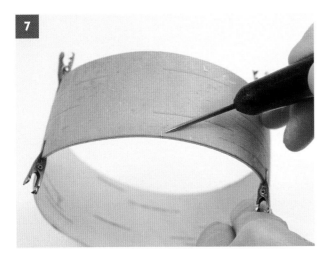

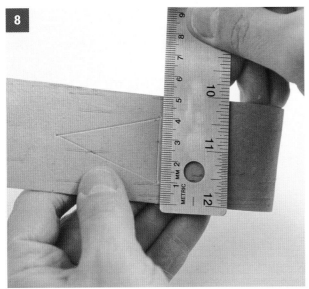

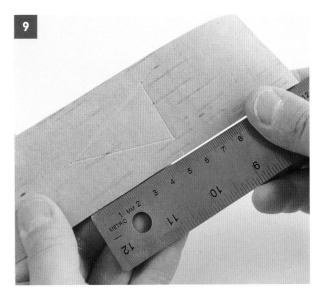

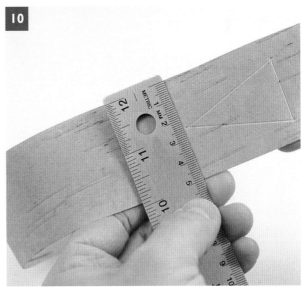

Make a mark approximately 2½ inches in from the left end of the collar (photo 7). Make the marks on both side edges of the overlapping strips of the collar (photo 7). The first mark is for the "tongue" on the (underlapped) end of the strip, and the second mark is for the triangular hole on the (overlapped) end of the strip.

The mark on the right end is the base of the triangular hole. Using the overlap mark on the right end of the collar (photo 7), make two marks with the point of an awl 1 cm in from each side on both (photo 8). Draw a line between these marks for the base of the triangle.

Note: *The measurements in parentheses that follow are for the top collar. If there is only one measurement, it applies to both collars.*

For the tip of the triangle, measure 5 cm (4 cm) to the left from the base of the triangle (photo 9) and make a mark in the middle at 2.5 cm (2 cm) (photo 10). Draw lines between each of these marks to delineate the triangle (photo 10).

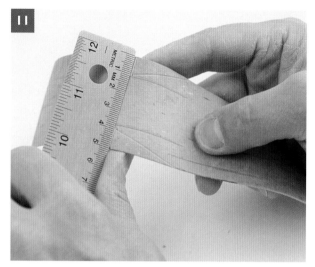

11

Keeping the strip in the same direction, go to the other end. This end is the part that will fit into the triangle to make the dovetail. Find the overlap mark. The base of each triangle measures 1 cm in from each edge, as shown here. Make the marks with your awl at the 1-cm points from both edges of the strip. Draw lines between each of these marks and each side of the strip to delineate the bases of the triangles.

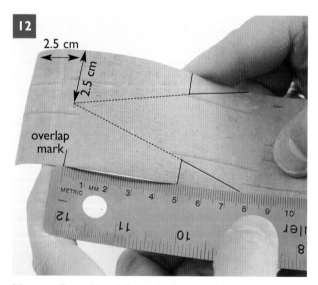

12

2.5 cm

2.5 cm

overlap mark

Measure 5 cm (4 cm) from the bases of the triangles to the left to find the point that will help to draw these two triangles that make up the "tongue."

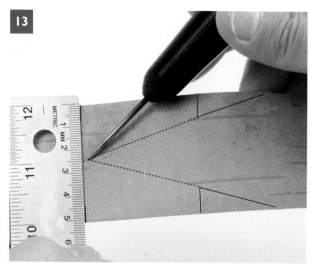

13

To draw the side triangles more accurately, place a ruler on the mark in the middle of the collar near the end extending to the 1-cm mark at the base of the triangle. Draw a line only from the base of the triangle to the outer edge of the collar. The dotted line indicates the placement of the ruler.

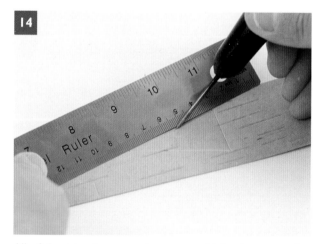

14

All of the triangles are to be cut out. Make deeper marks on all of the triangles with an awl (photo 14).

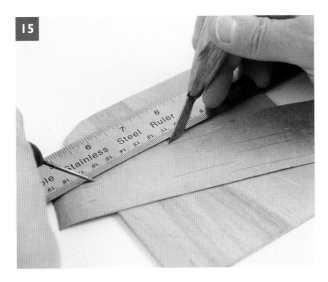

Then cut them out with a craft knife (photos 15–18). To keep from cutting too far, cut from the point of the triangle to within 5 mm of the base of the triangle, and then cut from the base back (photos 17–18). Do this with each of the edges. Do the same with the side triangles (photo 16).

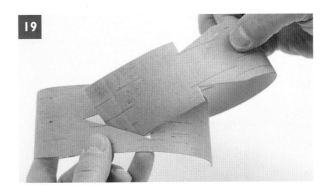

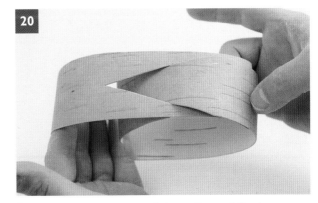

The tongue goes on top of the collar and fits into the triangular hole (photo 19). Photo 20 shows the completed dovetail.

To put the collar onto the cylinder, put them into hot (not boiling) water for only a few seconds.

Fold the cylinder into a kidney-bean shape so that the collar can be slipped over it and form a tight seal.

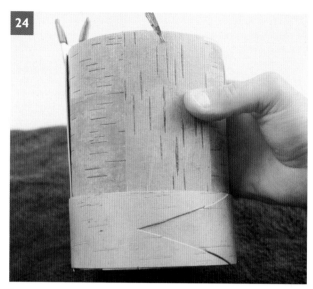

Form the cylinder into a round shape again. Here is the bottom collar in place.

After both of the collars are in place, trim the edges of the cylinder with a craft knife to make the edge even.

You can place the dovetails over one another, on different sides, or in different directions.

The bottom of the cylinder is made from fir. It measures the diameter of the cylinder plus 2 to 4 mm. The thickness of the bottom should be approximately 1 cm. Make the base fit by cutting off the edge with a knife (photo 26) and then sanding the edges smooth. Sand the bottom rim of the wooden base so that it will slip into the cylinder without damaging it.

Oil the inside of the cylinder from the halfway point down to the bottom to make it easier to slip the base into place.

Put the bottom of the cylinder into boiling water for just three to four seconds.

Slip the base in at a 30-degree angle (photos 31 and 32), and hammer it down flat with the handle of a hammer (photo 33). The base should be within approximately ⅜ inch from the bottom edge of the cylinder (photo 34).

Weaving the Canister Rim

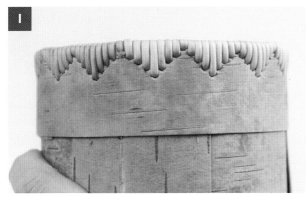

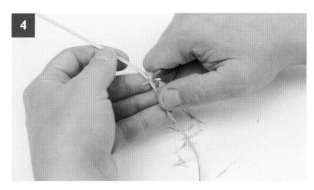

In traditional Novgorodian style, there is no additional strip added to the inside at the top. On this particular cylinder, the sewing forms a pyramid design.

Scrape off the pith to make the root even and smooth, as shown here. If necessary, cut off small branches and make the parts that are too thick or too wide narrower. You want to make the root as even and consistent as possible.

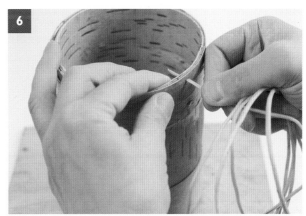

Soak the spruce roots in water to make them flexible (photo 2), and then split them in half lengthwise (photo 3).

Begin sewing the rim by making a hole with an awl 3 to 4 mm down from the top edge.

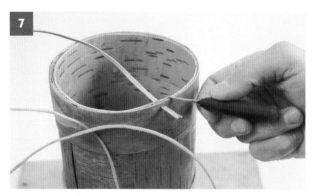

Thread the root into the hole from the outside to the inside, pulling it through until there is a 1 to 2-cm tail on the outside.

Make the next hole to the right 3 mm down.

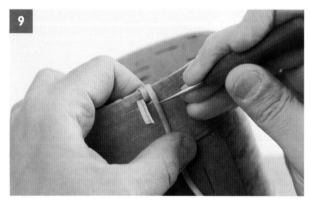

To make the pyramid design, make each successive hole 3 mm down from the last hole until there are five holes down. The design from there will be four holes up and four holes down.

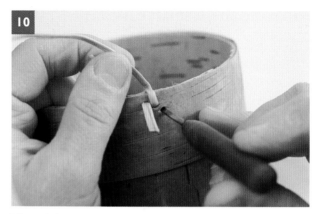

Thread the spruce root from the outside to the inside and pull tight.

Keep working four holes down and four holes up for the entire rim.

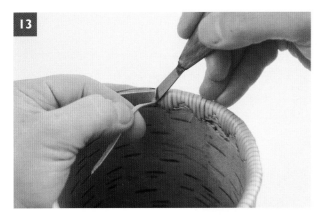

To add another root, cut off the old end inside.

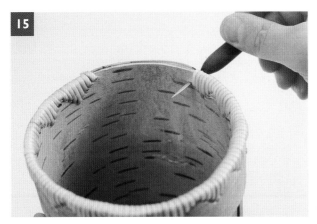

The new root goes in the same hole, so make the hole wider with your awl.

Keep your left thumb on the last stitch to keep the old root from pulling out when you take the awl out, and insert the new root in the hole from the outside to the inside. Leave a 1 to 2-cm tail on the new root.

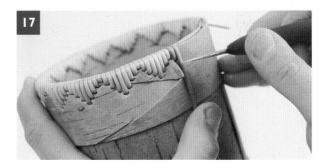

Resume sewing the next stitch with the new root.

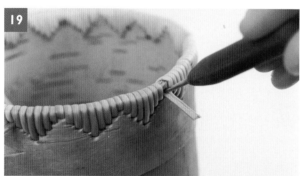

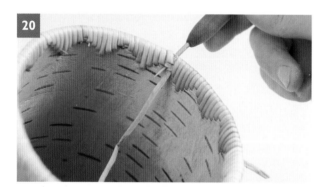

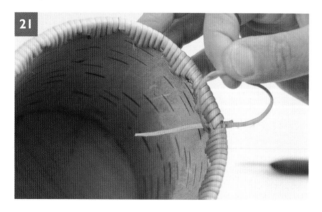

To end, thread the final end at an angle down through the same hole as the beginning end.

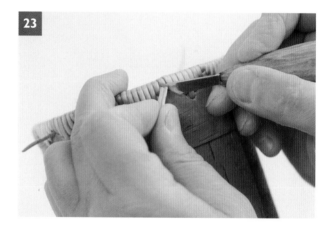

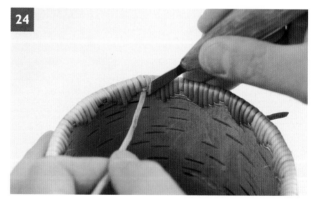

Cut the ends off flush with the outside (photo 23) and the inside of the rim (photo 24).

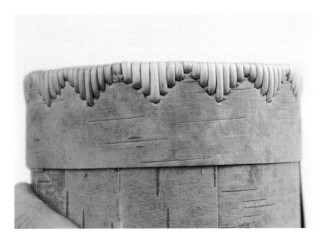

The finished rim.

MAKING THE CANISTER LID

Carve the lid and taper the edge so that it will go into the canister. Vladimir doesn't sand the lid. He likes to leave the knife marks.

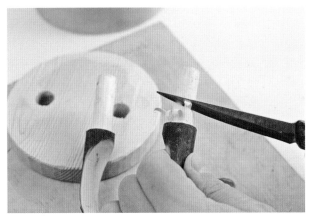

Drill two 12-mm holes 2½ inches apart in the top to accommodate the ends of the handle.

Making the Lid Handle

Carve the handle from thick willow. The length between the two cuts on each end that go into the lid is approximately 7½ inches. Carve the two cuts on each end that go into the lid a little wider than the diameter of the 12-mm holes. Boil it in water for two to three hours. Bend and form the handle around a bottle or similar object. Tie the ends on the form and let it dry for several days. When dry, carve with the knife around the ends of the handle to make them little smaller but just enough to put the ends of the handle through the holes in the lid so they fit very tight.

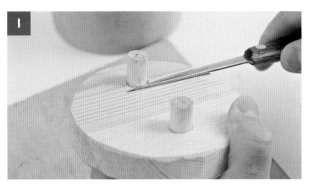

Make a mark on the inside edges of the handle under the lid. This is for the notches into which the wedge goes.

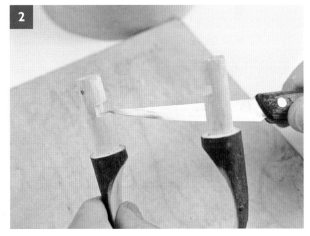

Carve the notch 5 mm wide and 3 to 4 mm deep.

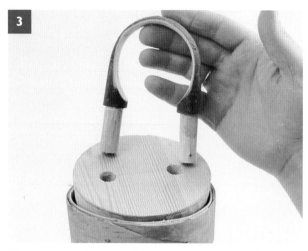

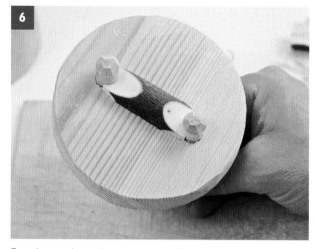

Carve the notches 1 to 1.5 mm deeper toward the top of the handle. The depth of this additional measurement of the notch will actually be hidden inside the lid. This helps to make the wedge fit tighter.

For the wedge, take a piece of willow that has been cut in half lengthwise (photo 4) and measures the length of the span between the ends, including the notches. Taper the ends so that they fit tightly in the notches (photo 5). Photo 6 shows the wedge in place.

Here the canister is being filled with water; note that there is no leakage!

project seventeen

Stamped, Sewn Rim with Embellishments

Weaving Level
intermediate to advanced

Dimensions
diameter 4¼ inches; height 9½ inches

Rim Materials
outside rim, 1 inch wide × 1 mm thick birch-bark strip the circumference of the basket plus a 2-inch overlap; inside rim, ⅝ inch wide × 1 mm thick birch-bark strip the circumference of the basket plus 1½ inches for the overlap; metal stamp (leather-embossing tools work well); 6½ to 8 feet of whole spruce roots, 2 to 3 mm wide

*T*his basket has been created with just one purpose: to show what kind of traditional decorations can be made on birch-bark baskets and to demonstrate how to make a sewn rim. The basket is diagonally plaited from a 10 × 10 base and is woven 15½ diamonds high. With the sewn rim and all of the embellishments, it makes a great conversation piece for those who would like to know about traditional Russian birch-bark basketry.

221

MAKING THE STAMPED, SEWN RIM
Stamping

Stamp the outer 1-inch-wide rim piece with the metal stamp lengthwise along the lower edge to make the embossed design.

Clamp the outer and inner rims onto the basket. First, clamp the outer rim on the basket beginning in a counterclockwise direction. Next, start the inner rim to the right of the beginning of the outer rim so that the overlap will end right where the inner rim begins.

Preparing the Roots

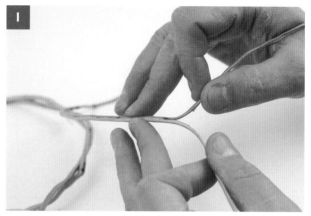

Prepare the spruce roots by soaking them in water and then splitting them lengthwise. Start the split with a knife, and then continue splitting with your fingers.

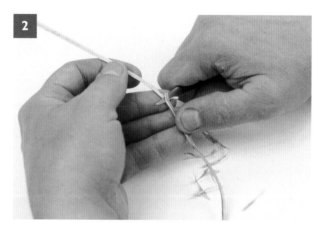

Scrape off the pith to make the root even and smooth, as shown here. If necessary, cut off small branches and make the parts that are too thick or too wide narrower. You want to make the root as even and consistent as possible.

Keep the roots wet while weaving. Every two or three stitches, wet your fingers and run them along the root to keep it supple.

Stitching the Rim

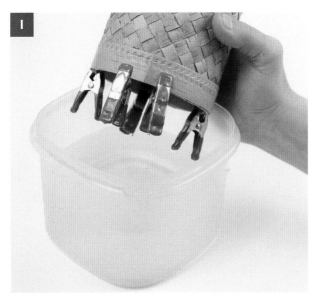

Invert the basket into a container of water to wet the rim before stitching.

Begin sewing the rim 1 1/2 inches to the right of the outside rim overlap, which is also the final edge of the inside overlap.

Make a hole with your awl 3 to 4 mm down from the top edge. This particular design is a sawtooth configuration. Don't go through the inner rim overlap at this point.

Run a pointed end of the spruce root into the hole (photo 4), and pull it completely through until a 3/8-inch tail shows on the outside (photo 5).

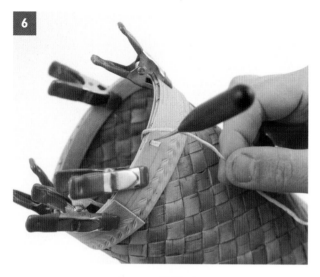

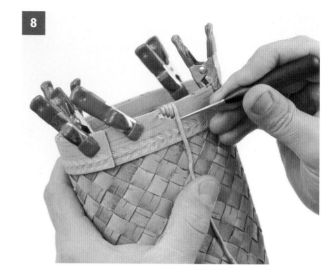

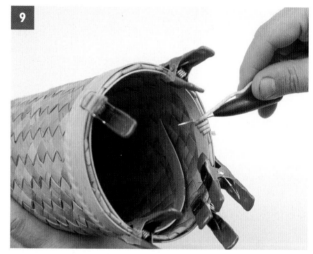

Make a hole to the right 2 mm down from the last one (photo 6), and thread the root into the hole from the outside. Pull tight on the inside (photo 7).

Make each successive hole 2 mm down from the last hole until there are five holes altogether. Photo 9 shows the fifth hole from the inside.

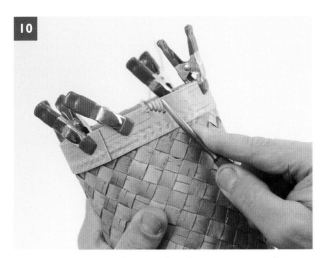

Push the roots together so that they remain totally vertical and compressed.

To add a new root, end the old one inside and trim it off flush.

Add a new root in the same hole underneath the old end, as shown here. Make the hole bigger with your awl. When you remove the awl, be sure to hold the last stitch so that it doesn't pull out.

Leave a 3⁄8-inch tail on the outside, and hold it down to the left so that it doesn't pull through, as shown here. Continue sewing as usual.

When you come to the inside rim overlap, incorporate the overlap in the sewing. Make sure the overlap is tight at this point. You don't want to have a gap between the rim and the body as you do the final stitching.

The End and Final Stitch

To end, cut off the beginning root end flush with the outside (photo 1). Make a hole with your awl slightly below the beginning end to avoid pushing the old end through. Sew the final stitch, leaving the end inside. Trim the end flush with the inside (photo 2).

Finishing Details

Make three stitches through the body up on a diagonal, and trim the ends of the root off with a craft knife.

Tack the outside overlap to finish off the rim. With your awl, make a hole ⅝ inch in from the vertical edge and ⅛ inch up from the bottom edge.

Trim the corner of the rim overlap off at a diagonal with a knife.

The finished rim.

EMBELLISHMENTS
Triangle Design

This triangle design zigzags from an upper diamond to a lower diamond around the basket. Each time you thread the strip through a diamond, it will be either oriented up to the right or down to the right.

With the underside of the strip up, thread it under a diamond that is oriented up to the right, as shown here. The left awl points to the beginning (photo 1).

Turn the strip up to the left and thread it, underside up, down through the next diamond marked with the right awl (photo 1).

At the bottom edge of the last diamond, turn the strip down to the left and thread it, underside up, through the lower diamond (photo 2). Repeat these two moves all the way around the basket, threading the final end through the first diamond under all the layers but above the beginning end of the strip. Trim the end with a craft knife.

Eyeglass Curls

The eyeglass-curls design can be made as a single row (photo 1) or a double row (photo 2).

Cut a ½-inch-wide strip in half lengthwise to make two ¼-inch strips. Thread it, underside up, through a diamond that is oriented up to the right (photo 1).

For making eyeglass curls, turn the strip down to the right, and thread it up under the next diamond (photo 1). Always keep the strip underside up during this threading. Pull it snug and flatten the loop with your awl. Continue around the basket in this manner, threading the final end through the first diamond under all the layers.

To make a counter design, thread another ¼-inch strip through a diamond that is oriented down to the right (photo 2). Turn the strip up to the right, and thread it down under the next diamond. Work as you did for the first row. Trim all ends with a craft knife.

Twisted Design

For a twisted design, each of the twists is done with a separate strip about 6 inches × ½ inch.

Thread one strip, right side up, through two diamonds to anchor it properly.

Turn it up under to the left to form a triangle; then bring the end, right side out, down to the right in preparation for threading it through two diamonds.

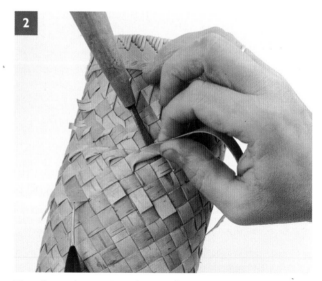

First, form the twist with your fingers.

3

Thread the end down through the next diamond, pulling it tight to keep the twist.

4

5

Thread the end down through a second diamond (photo 4). Photo 5 shows a basket with this design. Trim all the ends with a craft knife.

Three-Strand Braid

This three-strand braid is worked with three strips at once. Each of the strips zigzags around the basket intersecting in a braid fashion. The top half of the braid shows the right side of the strips; the lower half of the braid shows the underside of the strips.

Note: You can alter which side appears in specific locations by changing the side that is up when you insert the strip at the beginning.

1

Thread the first strip, underside up, through a diamond that is oriented up to the right. Leave a ¹/₂-inch end extending below the first diamond.

2

Bring the long end forward, fold it down at a right angle, and then thread it under the diamond that is oriented down to the right. Photo 2 also shows folding up the same strip at a right angle in preparation for threading it under the next diamond that is oriented up to the right.

Bring the same strip forward, fold it down at a right angle, and thread it under the next diamond that is oriented down to the right.

Add a second strip through the diamond to the right of the first strip.

Work the two strips so that they are facing up to the right.

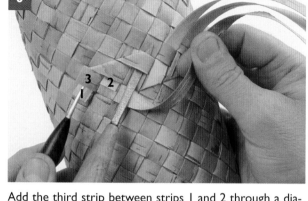

Add the third strip between strips 1 and 2 through a diamond that is facing down to the right.

Work the three strips up, then the three strips down (photo 7), all the way around (photo 8). Thread the final ends under all layers of the beginning diamonds but above the beginning end of the same strip. Trim the ends with a craft knife.

This braid can also be woven with each strip separately. Weave the first strip by itself and finish it off, then add the second strip and finish it off, and so forth.

Four-Strand Braid

This four-strand braid is worked in such a way that there is a diamond in the center of the braid.

Thread the first strip, underside up, under a diamond that is oriented up to the right.

Fold it down at a right angle, and thread it, right side up, through the next diamond.

Photo 1 shows folding the same strip up at a right angle in preparation for threading it up under the next diamond that is oriented up to the right.

Bring the same strip forward, fold it down at a right angle, and thread it under the next diamond that is oriented down to the right.

By folding each strip down over on the top part of the braid and up under on the lower part of the braid, the right side will be out in the middle throughout the entire braid.

Thread the second strip, underside up, under the next diamond to the right of the first one, as shown here. Fold and thread this second strip as you did for the first one.

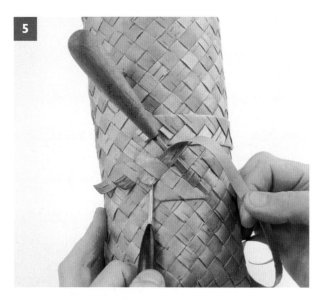

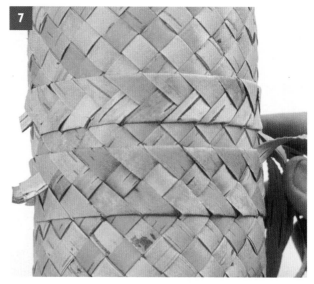

With each of the strips, in turn, continue folding down at a right angle, threading it through the next diamond, and then folding it up under at a right angle and threading through the next diamond around the entire basket. Thread each of the ends under the beginnings, going under all the layers but above the beginning end of the same strip. Trim the ends with a craft knife.

This braid also can be woven with each strip separately.

Five-Strand Braid

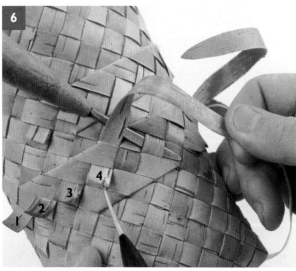

Working to the right, thread the third strip and the fourth strip under the diamonds in the same way.

Thread the first strip, underside up, under a diamond that is oriented up to the right.

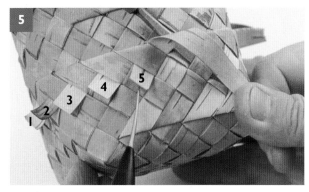

Fold the strip down at a right angle, and thread it, right side up, through the next two diamonds.

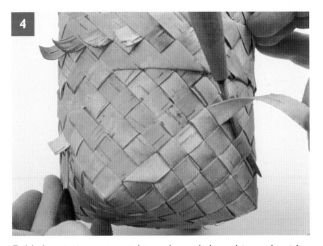

Fold the strip up at a right angle, and thread it, underside up, through the next two diamonds.

Thread strips 2, 3, 4, and 5, underside up, through the next four diamonds to the right.

With each of the five strips, in turn, continue the sequence established by the first strip around the entire basket. Thread each of the ends under the beginnings, going under all the layers. Trim the ends with a craft knife. This braid also can be woven with each strip separately.

Here is the finished triangle design worked on the center diamonds of the five-strand braid. This additional element is not traditional; it can give your basket a more contemporary look.

project eighteen

Oval Box with Pegs

Weaving Level
intermediate to advanced

Dimensions
base 4½ × 2½ inches; height 2¼ inches

Materials

1. birch-bark strips for weaving,
   1.5 mm thick (one in each length
   indicated below):
   • strip, 14 × 2 inches
   • strip, 11 × 2 inches
   • strip, 11¾ × 2 inches
   • strip, 13 × 1¼ inches
   • strip, 12¾ inches × ⅜ inch
2. piece of basswood for the lid,
   4 inches × 2½ inches × ⅜ inch
3. piece of basswood for the base,
   4 inches × 2½ inches × ½ inch
4. ⅛-inch dowel rod for pegs or pegs
   cut from a sturdy wood, such as birch
5. ⅛-inch dowel rod for the lid
6. 1 × 4 inch strip of sturdy leather
7. 12 inches of waxed linen or other
   strong thread

This kind of box can be seen almost everywhere that people create objects from birch bark. It is found in northwest Russia, in Siberia, in Scandinavian countries, and even in Alaska. It is traditionally made with only wooden pegs and no glue, which gives it a special charm and beauty. These boxes are customarily used for salt, tobacco, or small items.

On a personal note, we were looking for good sturdy leather for the handle on the lid, searching everywhere we could think of. Find it we did—in the form of an old boot in the middle of the highway in Berkeley, California! It proved to be the perfect weight.

The finished oval box with pegs.

WEAVING THE OVAL BOX

The form for making this basket is carved out of basswood and is 3¼ inches long × 1¾ inches wide × 4 inches tall.

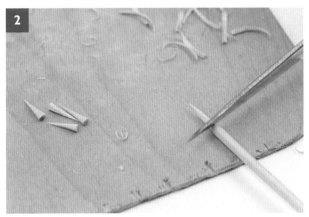

Make the pegs by whittling a ⅛-inch dowel rod to a point and then cutting them off at approximately ⁵⁄₁₆ inch, as shown here. Roll the dowel while cutting with a knife, holding the end down with your finger. Make four pegs ⅜ inch long for pegging the base.

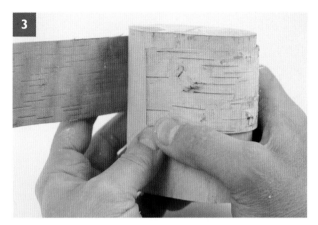

Starting halfway on the long side of the form, wrap the 14-inch-long piece tightly around with the underside of the bark out. This puts the right side inside, as shown here. This piece wraps around the form one and a half times.

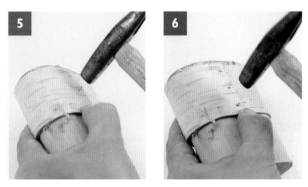

Make three evenly spaced holes with your awl along the edge of the overlap and hammer in the pegs.

Butt the second 2-inch-wide piece up against the edge of the first piece, except this time with the right side out. (From this point on, the rest of the pieces will have the right side of the bark facing out.) Hammer in two evenly spaced pegs along the edge, as shown in the photo.

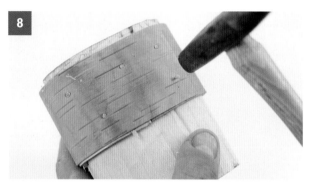

Wrap this piece around tightly, pegging in a zigzag configuration for the entire piece, as shown.

After the first two rows, the overlap on the additional strips is 1 to 2 inches.

Cut a zigzag pattern along both edges of the third (the 2-inch-wide) strip.

Hammer in two pegs along the butted edge of the zigzag piece (photo 10) as well as the end of that piece (photo 11).

Cut a zigzag pattern along both edges of the fourth (the 1¼-inch-wide) strip. Butt it up against the last strip, and secure it with one peg, as shown in the photo.

Peg the strip each inch all the way around along the center of the strip.

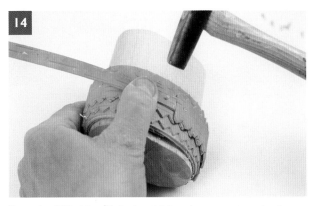

Butt the fifth (the ⅜-inch-wide) strip up against the last strip, and secure with one peg, as shown in the photo. Wrap it all the way around, pegging it every inch. Overlap the end about 1½ inches.

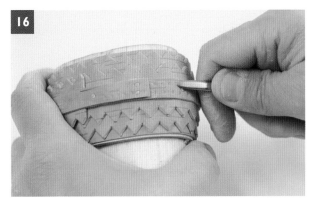

Cut the end off (photo 15) and secure with two pegs (photo 16). Emboss a design in the outer strip with your awl (photo 16).

Pull the basket off the mold. The pegs are soft enough to break free from the mold relatively easily.

Use a file to smooth off the tips of the pegs on the inside.

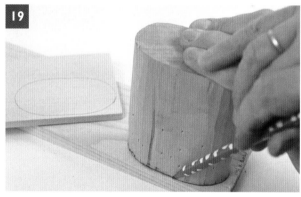

Half-inch-thick basswood is used for the base and the ⅜-inch-thick basswood for the lid. Draw an outline of the mold onto a piece of basswood, as shown here. Cut the base out 1½ mm wider than the outline and sand the edges. Oil the inside of the basket.

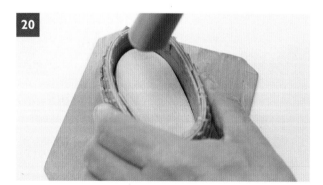

Put the base in at a 30-degree angle, and hammer it down with the handle of the hammer.

In order to peg the base, make the holes with your awl first.

Peg the base in four places (one on each end and one on each side) with ⅜-inch-long pegs.

Draw an outline of the mold on the second piece of basswood, and cut out the lid 1 ½ mm wider than the outline. Taper and sand the edges so that it will fit into the basket snugly.

For the lid handle, cut a piece of sturdy leather ¾ inch × 4 inches, as shown here. Taper the piece from the ⅝-inch width at the center to a point at each end so that the ends will slip into the slot easily.

Make a rectangular slot in the lid ¼ inch wide × ⅝ inch long. Drill a hole at each end of the slot, and then carve out the wood in between with a knife. File the slot smooth. Make sure the slot is big enough for the two ends of the leather to go through, also as shown here.

The finished oval box with pegs, showing the underside of the lid.

Slip both ends through the slot, making sure the loop extends ¾ inch above the top of the lid. On the underside of the lid, put an inch-long piece of ⅛-inch dowel rod, blunt-tipped at both ends, between the two ends of the leather handle right up against the lid. Wrap several times around the ends of the leather with waxed linen thread below the dowel. Tie the ends of the thread to hold the dowel in place, as shown in the photo. Cut the leather points off to ¼ inch below the waxed linen.

Part IV

Gallery of Plaited Baskets

When Craft Becomes Art

Braided Historical Musings

Bias or diagonal plaiting with birch bark is not intuitive. A novice basket maker, being given a handful of long, rectangular elements, will not on the first attempt, or even the one hundredth, be able to successfully weave a bias-plaited basket. He or she will eventually weave an over-and-under checkerboard placemat, and if a model basket is at hand, the novice will eventually figure out how to weave vertical sides. Finishing the rim will require some thought as to how to prevent it from unraveling, but the beginning weaver will undoubtedly accomplish it. This would be true for someone given any individual, long, rectangular, and flat weaving materials.

Cultures that have lived among palm trees are most likely to have discovered diagonal plaiting. Palm fronds, especially sword-palm fronds, like coconut palms, easily lend themselves to bias plaiting. On the palm frond, individual leaflets are attached to a great rib, extending from the frond's base to its tip. When split in half, the frond has a long, flexible woody base with dozens of individual leaflets, still attached, and all parallel to each other, perpendicular to the base. Interweaving these leaflets, by choosing adjacent pairs and interlacing them, becomes a simple task. The result is a diagonal plait.

It would be equally non-intuitive to ask a South Seas basket maker to make an Appalachian market basket with vertical spokes and horizontal weavers from a palm frond. However, weaving a diagonally plaited placemat and finishing the edges very neatly by weaving them back into the body of the mat would be relatively easy.

So how did bias or diagonal plaiting find its way into the birch forests of Finland and northwestern Russia at least by the thirteenth century? Some evidence suggests that bias plaiting might already have been used in weaving lapti from the inner bark of the linden tree in rural villages. But the question of origin still remains.

A vast network of Eurasian trade existed well before the time of the Roman Empire. Among other evidence for this, as early as the sixth century B.C.E., domestic Chinese silk was found in the tomb of a

Celtic prince in Hochdorf in southern Germany. Of course, spices and other commodities were brought from the East in exchange for furs, amber, and other necessities found in the North. All of these commodities were packaged for transport by workers, slaves, or draught animals as well as by water routes. Heavy, breakable pottery would not always have been the packaging material of choice. Heavy tapestries could serve double duty as cushioning and later be sold, but lightweight baskets were undoubtedly functional as a major means of containment.

In medieval times, sea trade existed throughout the Indian Ocean from the Moluccas and the Malay archipelago, Burma and India, to the Persian Gulf where goods were then picked up by Arabs who transported them to the Black Sea where they were exchanged with Vikings for carriage farther north. Eventually, we could speculate, that's how plaited cane and bamboo baskets from South East Asia must have become available throughout the European continent.

I can imagine a bitterly cold night and people huddled in a shelter with birch bark covering both walls and ceiling. The bark has been delaminating as is common. Then a craftsman, perhaps possessing or remembering an Asian basket recently seen in the marketplace, starts to pull strips of bark off the wall and begins to play. Perhaps he even consciously attempts to duplicate the bamboo weaves he has seen. Carefully studying the basket from the Far East, he tries to decipher the unusual corners and the upset for the basket's sides.

Plaiting is indeed an intellectual exercise as well as a craft that requires still more concentration than coiling, twining, or plain weaving, while still providing the easy interplay of fingers and materials with the rhythmic repetition of elements interlacing. When plaiting, all elements are active. There is no static warp or foundation with which the active weft or sewing element must interlace. Along with this intense concentration, plaiting can result in spectacular shapes and forms—whether geometric, architectural, animal, or human. Jack Lenor Larsen, world-renowned textile and fabric designer, defines plaiting as fabrics "interlaced with one or more sets of elements. These include interlacings that are oblique, horizontal-vertical, spiral, multidirectional, or some combination of these."

Because the only requirement for plaiting is that the elements should be flat and long, an abundant variety of materials can be chosen for plaiting. Even if you have no access to birch bark, strips of metal, wooden splints, flat reeds, bamboo and rattan strips, and even strapping tape found by dumpster-diving can serve. Several artists in this gallery use heavy watercolor paper, first painting it, then cutting it into long strips before plaiting the strips into their artwork. Another artist cuts road maps into strips, while still another chose exposed 35-mm film as her weaving element.

—Jim Widess

Weaving Materials

ash splints
bamboo
barks
brass sheets
candy wrappers
cane
cardboard
cedar bark
coconut palm fronds
computer paper with perforated edges
copper sheets
elm bark
film
flax leaves
grocery bags
juice boxes
kraft paper
lauhala
leather
magazine pages
metals in pliable strips
newspaper
oak splints
palm leaves
paper currency
plastic strapping tape
rattan
reeds, flat and flat-oval shapes
ribbon, especially grosgrain
road maps
rushes
swamp ash
watercolor paper
willow bark
yucca

Using Materials other than Birch Bark

Birch bark, while beautiful, flexible, waterproof, and enduring, is not readily available to most basket weavers. Luckily, the plaiting techniques found in Part II, "Weaving and Basketry Basics" (general directions), and used in the eighteen projects of Part III, "Plaited Basketry Projects," can be worked successfully with other traditional or contemporary materials. Here in Part IV, "Gallery of Plaited Baskets," you will find many baskets made from various flat and flexible materials: watercolor and drawing papers; magazine covers; copper strips or other pliable metal strips; plastic strapping tape; folded newspaper or kraft paper (made from wood pulp); film strips; lauhala with any thorns trimmed; barks such as elm, willow, and cedar; coconut palm-frond leaflets; New Zealand flax leaves; shredded money or currency cut into strips; road maps; candy wrappers laminated and cut into strips; juice boxes; PVC tape; ribbon; and lightweight cardboard.

A Few Hints

Here are some hints for making plaited baskets like those shown in these pages. Papers, such as 140# watercolor paper and 80# drawing paper, can be painted with acrylics on both sides. Cut them either with a rotary cutter or craft knife to make the strips the required size or run them through a pasta machine to make ¼-inch (0.75 cm) strips.

Because newspaper and kraft paper are not as sturdy, try folding them several times to make them more stable and easier to weave.

Tooling copper, the kind used for repoussé, available through various art-supply catalogs, is thin enough to be cut with a pasta machine, paper cutter, or rotary cutter. The copper needs to be stretched and straightened to make it stiff enough for weaving. This can be accomplished by clamping one end of a strip in a vise and pulling with a pair of pliers from the other end. During the weaving process, the copper may, however, become "work-hardened," or stiff, and even brittle. If this happens, you can heat the copper with a torch to anneal and relax it so that it can again be woven. Heating also adds interesting color variations to the copper, which can become another design element.

Note: Photos in the gallery are by Jim Widess, unless otherwise noted.

Linda Sura

Linda Sura plaits baskets from painted cold-press watercolor paper. She lives in south Texas.

Brown Mica, Linda Sura.

Red Sky at Night, Linda Sura.

Forest Edge, Linda Sura.

Red, White, and Blue, Linda Sura.

Donna Carlson

Donna Carlson creates sewn birch-bark containers, which she then embellishes with natural and dyed porcupine quills in the northeastern Native North American Micmak style.

Escher, Donna Carlson.

Dogwood, Donna Carlson.

Impatiens, Donna Carlson.

Pansy, Donna Carlson.

Jane Patrick

Jane Patrick, former editor for Handwoven magazine, is a lifelong weaver and author of the book *Time to Weave: Simply elegant projects to make in almost no time* (2006). Photos pages 246–247 by Jane Patrick.

Australia Simpson Desert, woven from pages of an atlas.

Funny-Papers Basket, woven from newsprint and finished with diluted white glue.

Bead Basket, handmade paper with wooden and glass beads, secured with embroidery floss, Jane Patrick.

Flower-Wallpaper Basket, Jane Patrick. The artist cut wallpaper sample book paper into ½-inch strips for this basket.

Paper-Bag Basket, woven from brown grocery bags, with a folded edge, Jane Patrick.

Handmade-Paper Basket, Jane Patrick. Handmade paper was used to weave this basket.

"Read All About It," woven from newspaper want ads and finished with beeswax, Jane Patrick.

Tape-and-Brad Basket, Jane Patrick. To make the weavers for this basket, the artist first sprinkled parchment paper with red and blue glitter; then placed white $1/2$-inch tape on top. She then cut the paper along the tape lines for weavers with parchment on one side and tape on the other side, with glitter sandwiched in between.

Teresa Tekulve

Teresa Tekulve collects birch bark and creek dog-wood shoots from around her home in Montana to create contemporary-looking baskets using age-old sewing techniques.

Carol Hart

Carol Hart weaves bleached-and-dyed Hamburg cane following the river-cane tradition of the Cherokee and Chitimacha Native North Americans of the Southeast.

Double-woven cane basket, Carol Hart.

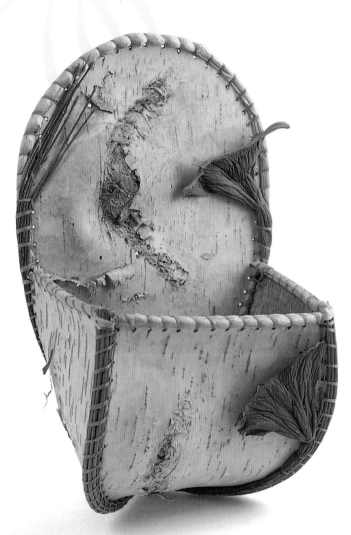

Birch wall basket, made from birch bark, creek dogwood, philodendron sheath, and imitation sinews, Teresa Tekulve.

Flo Hoppe

After being steeped in birch-bark basketry techniques from writing general and project instructions for this book, co-author Flo Hoppe has come to feel that the diagonal-plaiting and double-woven techniques are magical! When she weaves birch bark or painted paper into little squares or diamonds, turns the corners up, plaits the sides, folds down the rim, and threads the strips down the sides and bottom, she is always amazed and delighted at the finished product, for both its strength and its beauty. As she explores and experiments with other weaving materials, Flo applies what she has learned from birch-bark plaiting.

Cardboard tote, made from cardboard, acrylic paint, and plastic lacing, Flo Hoppe. The tote measures 8 × 5 × 3 inches. Photo by John C. Keys.

Two cardboard baskets, Flo Hoppe. The one on the left is 7 inches square and 9 inches high, and the one on the right is 5 ½ inches square and 7 inches high. Photo by John C. Keys.

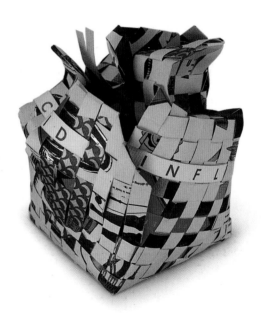

Classic Laid Influences, made with paper from a paper company brochure, Flo Hoppe. The basket measures 5 × 5 × 6 inches. Photo by John C. Keys.

Flo Hoppe (continued)

Aso-Zan, made from Japanese handmade paper, bamboo, and raffia, Flo Hoppe. The basket measures 10 inches × 4½ inches × ¾ inch. Photo by John C. Keys.

Kyushu, made with Japanese handmade paper, Flo Hoppe. The basket measures 10 × 4 × 10¾ inches. Photo by John C. Keys.

Ripples, made with watercolor paper, Flo Hoppe.

Basket with sawtooth rim, made with watercolor paper, Flo Hoppe.

Treasure box, made with watercolor paper, Flo Hoppe.

Lapti, made with watercolor paper, Flo Hoppe.

Jackie Abrams

Jackie Abrams makes contemporary-looking baskets and lives in the Northeast. "Bias plaiting is an incredibly versatile technique," she says. With bias plaiting, "I can weave baskets that are sculptural or symmetrical, with graceful curves or angular shoulders, with feet or double walls." While she generally uses heavy cotton paper because it is flexible, "Just about anything is possible," she says.

Rasta Flaps, Jackie Abrams. Photo by Jeff Baird.

Sculptural/Asymmetrical, Jackie Abrams. This asymmetrical basketry sculpture measures 6 × 11 × 8 inches. Photo by Jeff Baird.

Blue Ode, with double walls, Jackie Abrams. The basket measures 4 × 11 × 11 inches. Photo by Jeff Baird.

Lilac Star, Jackie Abrams. The basket measures 4 × 8 × 8 inches. Photo by John Douglas.

Two Sisters, Jackie Abrams. The piece measures 15 inches square × 12 inches high. Photo by Jeff Baird.

Blocks, Jackie Abrams. Photo by Jeff Baird.

Judith Saunders

Judith Saunders creates contemporary baskets and lives in Virginia. She explains the pivotal role that two of her teachers, Shereen and David LaPlantz, played in the development of her weaving. "I signed up for a class with David called 'Cold Connections in Metals.' I was teaching a jewelry class in a room with no ventilation, and, for health reasons, needed alternatives to soldering. I needed another class and signed up for Shereen's plaited basketry class. I really had no idea what distinguished plaiting from other forms of basketry. I was lucky to have worked with both David and Shereen and to see the possibility of overlapping metals and weaving in my work."

While Judith loves the effect she can achieve with copper, she finds it easier to work with more pliable materials. She has most enjoyed plaiting with different kinds of paper.

Blue Ice, made with plaited watercolor paper, Judith Saunders.

Plaited and Pleated, made with plaited watercolor paper, Judith Saunders.

Diamonds × Four, made with plaited watercolor paper, Judith Saunders.

Spiral, If You Dare, made with plaited copper, Judith Saunders.

Asymmetrical Venture, made with plaited copper, Judith Saunders.

Standing Tall, made with plaited copper, Judith Saunders.

Tiny Treasures, Itty-Bitty Bias, made with plaited copper, Judith Saunders.

Ed Rossbach

Ed Rossbach, considered the father of contemporary basketry by many textile artists, became enamored with plaiting techniques during the 1970s. He appreciated the quick weaving afforded by plaiting, the variety of materials he could utilize, and the continuous shapes that could be a canvas for his surface embellishments. Photos pages 256–257 by Ed Rossbach.

Plaited-lauhala basket, with stenciled embellishment, Ed Rossbach. The basket measures 5 × 5 × 12 inches.

Ash splint basket, with stenciled embellishments, Ed Rossbach. The basket measures 6 × 6 × 12 inches.

Ash splint basket, with painted image, Ed Rossbach. The basket measures 8 × 8 × 8 inches.

Basket made with fabric-covered paper, Ed Rossbach. The basket measures 6 × 6 × 10 inches.

Basket made with birch bark, staples, raffia, and flat reed, Ed Rossbach. The basket measures 9 × 3 × 3 inches.

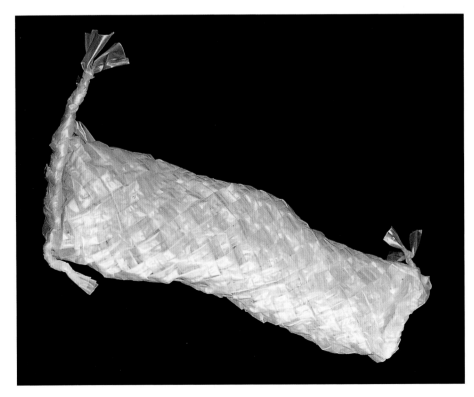

Basket made with plaited vinyl tubing, Ed Rossbach. The basket measures 12 × 4 × 3 inches.

Lorraine Oller

Lorraine Oller, a contemporary basket maker living in the San Francisco Bay Area, likes plaiting with painted paper strips. She says that's because first she gets to enjoy messing with paint on a big sheet of paper and then she gets to cut it up and transform it into something else.

Film Noir, made with 16-mm and 8-mm film, Lorraine Oller.

Basket made from watercolor paper with acrylic red, gray, and black paint, Lorraine Oller.

Basket made from watercolor paper with acrylic orange and blue paint, Lorraine Oller.

Film Noir (bottom of the basket), Lorraine Oller.

Southeast Asia and Pacific Islands

Here are plaited baskets from the eastern Pacific Rim and Southeast Asia, from the collection of Sher Widess. The artists are unknown.

Lauhala basket, origin uncertain. From the collection of Sher Widess.

Bamboo plaited basket from China. From the collection of Sher Widess.

Rattan pack basket from Borneo. From the collection of Sher Widess.

Lauhala basket from Samoa. From the collection of Sher Widess

Plaited bamboo basket from the Philippines. From the collection of Sher Widess.

Cass Schorsch

Michigan artist and birch-bark basketry teacher Cass Schorsch harvests birch bark in late spring for her classes in the United States and Canada in the coming year. After harvesting, she tediously prepares strips by splitting, waxing, and cutting the bark into strips ¼ inch or narrower.

Self-taught, Cass adapted her knowledge of black ash preparation to that of birch bark. Her challenge came in determining what technique to use with birch bark that did not need to be wet during the weaving process. She consulted Shereen LaPlantz's books to teach herself bias-plaiting and found this the most rewarding technique. If the bark was a bit thin, it did not matter because bias-plaiting is double-walled. Cass is co-author of a book on natural baskets. She loves the finished baskets and the experience of weaving with birch bark.

Her work has been exhibited in numerous juried shows and appeared in books. Her one-woman show was sponsored by the Boston Arts & Crafts Society in 2005 and her work is found in the permanent collection of the Michigan State Museum.

ABOVE: *Poncho for Sedona,* birch bark and copper, Cass Schorsch. Photo by Cass Schorsch.

LEFT: *Copper Kitten,* made from birch bark and copper, Cass Schorsch. Photo by Cass Schorsch.

Turning Corners, made from birch bark, Cass Schorsch. Photo by Cass Schorsch.

Stray Cat, made from birch bark and copper, Cass Schorsch. Photo by Cass Schorsch.

Warm and Hearty, clear and stained birch bark, Cass Schorsch. Photo by Cass Schorsch.

Miscellaneous birch-bark rattles, Cass Schorsch. Photo by Cass Schorsch.

Prasert Sytha

Laotian-American artist Prasert Sytha made the two rice baskets shown from dumpster-diving in which he collected and recycled yellow strapping tape.

Two rice baskets, made with recycled strapping tape, using bamboo basket plaiting techniques, Prasert Sytha. From the collection of Sher Widess.

Lai Sivalay

The artist Lai Sivaly moved to the San Francisco Bay Area from Laos after the Vietnam War. Lai takes advantage of the delta of nearby Stockton and his Laotian community, where a plot of timber bamboo grows that can be harvested for making rice baskets.

Classic bamboo plaited basket on bamboo stilts decorated with colored marking pens, Lai Sivalay.

Vladimir Yarish

Vladimir thinks *shkatulki* ("small boxes for keeping valuables") and *tabakerki* ("snuffboxes") are interesting because of the way they are made from birch-bark sheets. These small containers are constructed with several layers of birch bark. The outer layers were often decorated along the edge with marks resembling teeth, although these marks were generally made with a kostyk. They have a wooden bottom and lid. All birch-bark layers, even the bottom layer, are strengthened with wooden pins.

Oval box with wooden pegs, Vladimir Yarish.

Oval baskets stitched with roots, Vladimir Yarish.

Round containers with feet, Vladimir Yarish.

Vladimir Yarish (continued)

Rattles and Balls

Through the centuries in Russia, children have played with *sharkunki* ("rattles") and balls. These were woven square items that differed only in size. Sometimes balls made in this fashion were wrapped in rags for durability. The rattles were frequently given a wooden handle, and they were filled with dried beans or peas to make noise.

Dolls

In the mid-20th century, people began making birch-bark dolls and animals just for fun. Some fashioned them for shows while others made them for children.

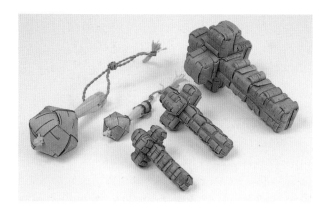

Rattles, Vladimir Yarish.

Large birch-bark rattle with a carved wooden handle and a linden-bark braid adorned with yarn fringe, Vladimir Yarish.

Folk dolls, Vladimir Yarish.

Market baskets, Vladimir Yarish.

Baskets and Shoulder Bags

Baskets and shoulder bags were distinguished by their size and diversity. There are many *lukoshki* ("peasant housekeeping baskets without handles") and several satchels on display at the Novgorod State Museum of History, Architecture, and Fine Arts. The shoulder bags used for gathering berries and mushrooms were made with two woven or rope straps and could be used as a knapsack, carried on the back. Some satchels were made in the shape of a box and had a single shoulder strap. Other types were more like baskets but flatter and had an open top; these satchels had two strong, linden-bark "rope" handles, much like today's shopping bags.

Shepherd's bag, Vladimir Yarish.

Basket with root-decorated rim, Vladimir Yarish.

Vladimir Yarish *(continued)*

Containers

Various containers, such as saltcellars, canisters, grain and other bottles, hinged-lid boxes, and round storage boxes traditionally have been made with birch bark.

Woven container, Vladimir Yarish. Photo by Judy Kramer.

Double-cylinder canister, Vladimir Yarish. Photo by Judy Kramer.

One-cylinder canister, Vladimir Yarish.

Grain bottle, Vladimir Yarish.

Bottle with carved top, Vladimir Yarish.

Woven canister, Vladimir Yarish.

Hinged-lid boxes,
Vladimir Yarish.

Round box with pegs, wooden lid, and
roots, Vladimir Yarish. The box's diameter
is 8 inches and its height 4 inches.

Vladimir Yarish (continued)

The Rozhok, a Musical Instrument

In Russia today, very few shepherds make and use the *rozhok* (the local Novgorodian name for the *zhaleika*), a traditional wind musical instrument. The rozhok consists of an alder or willow branch (twig) made into a hollow cylinder about 6 to 8 inches long that has two to five sound holes that can be played with the fingers to create different notes. At one end is a bell-shaped "horn" made of many layers of wrapped birch-bark with the yellowy inner bark facing out. At the other end is the so-called reed which the mouth played by blowing.

Shepherds usually only knew about two folk tunes, one played early morning while taking cows or sheep to pastures or woodlands from the courtyard and another when driving them home at night. At gatherings, shepherds from nearby villages played to one another. And when distant, the rozhok of a neighbor could be heard up to two or three miles away. Another shepherd might respond with his own tune. For another example of the rozhok, author Vladimir Yarish is shown holding one in his photo on page 277.

Hunting Call, a musical instrument, Vladimir Yarish.

Just for Tea

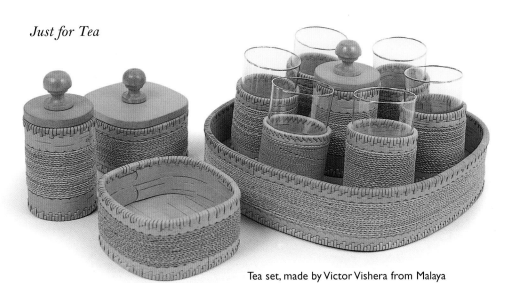

Tea set, made by Victor Vishera from Malaya Vishera in Novgorod province.

Tea-glass holder, Vladimir Yarish.

Wearables and Accessories

Stupni, Vladimir Yarish.

Birch-bark boots, Vladimir Yarish.

Clutch purse with woven-in handle, Vladimir Yarish.

Eyeglass case, Vladimir Yarish.

Vladimir Yarish (continued)

Birch-Bark Necklaces

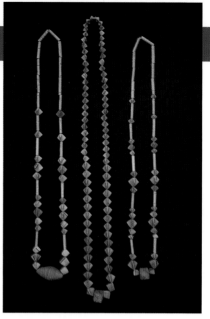

Three necklaces made with birch-bark beads, Vladimir Yarish.

Birch-bark necklace with two stacked diamond-shaped pendants, Vladimir Yarish.

Birch-bark necklace with cylinder, pentagonal, and cube-shaped beads, Vladimir Yarish.

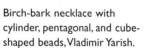

Birch-bark necklace with cylinder, pentagonal, and cube-shaped beads with looped pendant, Vladimir Yarish.

A Basket Weaver's Glossary with Russian Terms

banya Russian bath house.

bashmak Another word for *stupen* (see below). The plural is bashmaki.

bast Inner fiber of linden bark. It was used in medieval Novgorod as a fiber or thread for stitching parts of birch bark or for making rope or cords. Another word for bast material is *mochalo*. Bast is also a very good material for weaving *lapti* ("shoes"), shepherd's and fishermen's bags, baskets, and so forth.

bereshchenik Woven birch-bark shoes, which Russians call *lapot* or *stupen*. The plural is bereshcheniki.

berestenechka Derived from the word *beresta* ("birch bark") and means a birch-bark box for store something—butter, for example. The plural is *berestenechki*.

churback Piece of a log; part of a tree trunk. The plural is *churbachki*.

gorlatka Bottle-shaped basket. From the word *gorlo* ("throat"). The plural is *gorlatki*.

grabelki Small garden rake.

korob A large enough birch-bark box or wooden box for storing something in a house. The plural is *koroba*.

kostyk (kostik) Special weaving tool made of wood, bone, or forged iron. The plural is *kostyki*.

lapot Woven shoes of plant material (birch bark, linden bark, elm bark, and so forth). The plural is *lapti*.

lopatka Small wooden trowel to help in harvesting birch bark. The plural is *lopatki*.

lub Word for both linden tree bark and elm tree bark.

lukoshko Peasant housekeeping basket without a handle. Basket for collecting mushrooms or berries in the forest, for example. The plural is *lukoshki*.

Mesolithic The cultural period 15,000 years ago between the Paleolithic and Neolithic ages. The bow and cutting tools were invented during this period.

mochalka Derived from *mochalo* and means bast whisk for bathing. (*Bannaya mochalka* means "bast whisk for bathing.")

muzhik Russians use the word *muzhik* (*moujik*, *muzjik*, or *mujik*) or "peasant" to signify villagers and people who live in the country as distinct from city folk. It does not have the pejorative connotation it might have in the West.

Neolithic The cultural period beginning around 10,000 B.C.E. in the Middle East. During this period, farming was invented as were technically advanced stone tools.

Oblast Province in Russia.

Paleolithic The cultural period starting 750,000 years ago, when the earliest chipped stone tools were discovered, and ending at the beginning of the Mesolithic age.

pazilo From the verb *pazit*, "to make a groove in a log in constructing houses." *Pazilo* has the same meaning as *lopatka* (see above).

peasant See *muzhik*.

plaiting A form of weaving or interlacing in which single elements or sets of elements of the same width and flexibility pass over and under each other, usually at right angles. The weaving or interlacing can be worked on a horizontal/vertical axis or diagonally.

pood Russian measure for weight equal to 16.2 kilograms or 36 pounds.

rubashka shirt (or jacket); outer layer of the *tues*, which fits around the cylinder, which is the inner part of the *tues*.

sapog High boots. The plural is *sapogi*.

shchemyalka Clip to hold strips during weaving. The plural is *shchemyalki*.

shkatulka Casket, small fine box for keeping treasures. The plural is *shkatulki*.

shpilka Wooden peg used for stitching layers of birch bark in making boxes with solid sheets of bark. The plural is *shpilki*.

skoloten Birch-bark cylinder pulled from a tree in one piece. The plural is *skolotni*.

sochalka (sochilka) Special tool used for harvesting birch-bark cylinders. It is a long, metal, flat, approximately 6-mm wire that you insert between the wood and the birch bark to split the bark off the wood. In the Novgorod area, this word means "to remove or pull off the bark from a tree." The root of the word, *sok* ("juice"), means "the sapwood of a tree (the external layer of young wood adjoining the bark)."

stupen (bereshcheniki or **khodoki)** Birch-bark shoes without ropes used as galoshes. The plural is *stupni*.

tabakerka Box for keeping tobacco. The plural is *tabakerki*.

tues Birch-bark vessel, usually round, used primarily for liquids. The plural is *tuesi*.

vedyorko Epithet for pail from the word *vedro*, which means "pail."

yazychok Literally "little tongues" (plural). A part of the outer layer of the sheet of birch bark where the ends interlock to form a cylindrical shape. See *Zamok*. The plural is *yazychki*.

zamok Kind of lock for interlocking the ends of the outer layer of the bark to produce a canister. The plural is *zamki*.

Metric Equivalents

Figures are rounded off to the nearest mm, 0.1 cm, or 0.01 mm.

Inches	Millimeters	Centimeters
⅛	3	0.3
¼	6	0.6
⅜	10	1.0
½	13	1.3
⅝	16	1.6
¾	19	1.9
⅞	22	2.2
1	25	2.5
1¼	32	3.2
1½	38	3.8
1¾	44	4.4
2	51	5.1
2½	64	6.4
3	76	7.6
3½	89	8.9
4	102	10.2
4½	114	11.4
5	127	12.7
6	152	15.2
7	178	17.8
8	203	20.3
9	229	22.9
10	254	25.4
11	279	27.9
12	305	30.5
13	330	33.0
14	356	35.6
15	381	38.1
16	406	40.6
17	432	43.2
18	457	45.7
19	483	48.3
20	508	50.8
21	533	53.3
22	559	55.9
23	584	58.4

Inches	Millimeters	Centimeters
24	610	61.0
25	635	63.5
26	660	66.0
27	686	68.6
28	711	71.1
29	737	73.7
30	762	76.2
31	787	78.7
32	813	81.3
33	838	83.8
34	864	86.4
35	889	88.9
36	914	91.4
37	940	94.0
38	965	96.5
39	991	99.1
40	1016	101.6
41	1041	104.1
42	1067	106.7
43	1092	109.2
44	1118	111.8
45	1143	114.3
46	1168	116.8
47	1194	119.4
48	1219	121.9
49	1245	124.5
50	1270	127.0

Conversion Factors

1 mm = 0.039 inch

1 inch = 2.54 cm = 25.4 mm

1 foot = 12 inches = 30.48 cm = 304.8 mm

1 square foot = 0.09 m^2

1 meter = 39 inches = 3.28 feet

1 yard = 3 feet = 36 inches

1 square meter = 10.8 square feet

Abbreviations

mm: millimeter, **cm:** centimeter, **m:** meter

Index

About the Authors

Vladimir Yarish, a master, award-winning basket maker, has worked with birch bark for over 24 years. Born in Qaraghandy, Kazakhstan, Vladimir moved to Novgorod province. He has been teaching birch-bark basketry at his studio in the Cultural Palace of the city Velikiy Novgorod, since 1993. Beginning in 1997, Vladimir has been invited to teach classes in various locales in the United States. He has published many articles on birch-bark and traditional basket-making for both academic journals and popular magazines. He is currently researching the history of traditional birch-bark basketry, haunting, as permitted, every relevant museum and archeological site in Russia.

His works have been featured in the Hamburg Museum of Ethnology, the Saint Petersburg Toy Museum, and the Novgorod State Museum of Architecture, History, and Fine Arts. He has participated in numerous exhibitions and won awards at home and abroad for his basket-making talents. He lives with his wife Tatiana and son George.

Flo Hoppe is an artist, teacher, and author. Her specialties are wicker (round reeds) and Japanese basketry. She lived in Japan from 1968 to 1971, and more recently she has studied with two Japanese master basket makers in Tokyo. She is the author of *Wicker Basketry* (Sterling, 1999) and *Contemporary Wicker Basketry* (Lark, 1997). The latter title has been translated into German, *Fletchen mit Peddigrhor* (Paul Haupt, Bern, 1998). Flo teaches and exhibits worldwide, and she has been a contributor to other books on basketry. She lives in upstate New York with her husband Don.

Jim Widess has owned The Caning Shop in Berkeley, California, since 1971. He has had a prolific career as an author, with ten books to his credit. He is the author of *Gourd Pyrography* (2002) and co-author with Ginger Summit of *The Complete Book of Gourd Craft* (1996), *Making Gourd Musical Instruments* (2000), *The Complete Book of Gourd Carving* (2004), and *Making Gourd Dolls & Spirit Figures* (2007), all published by Sterling. Jim not only organized and developed these titles, contacting and working with over 400 contributing artists, but he has taken the bulk of photographs, whether for the books' step-by-step instructions or photo galleries. He began work on *Plaited Basketry with Birch Bark* in the late 1990s and has taken over 3,000 photos, which have been culled for this book. He has studied basketry with various teachers, including Flo Hoppe. He is also the author of *The Complete Guide to Chair Caning* (Lark, 2006) and *How to Weave Hawaiian Coconut Palm Fronds* (Mutual, 2006). Jim has a zeal for visual instructions for crafts and likes Hawaiian shirts. He lives in northern California with his wife Sher and teenage son Andy.

Woven bird, Vladimir Yarish.

Acknowledgments

When I was first shown how to weave birch bark back in 1984, all I wanted to do was make a few traditional baskets. When I established my studio in 1993 to teach basketry, I learned how to weave more contemporary baskets. Upon coming to the United States for the first time, I saw a lot of weaving styles—traditional, contemporary, avant-garde—and returned home with a headache. But, on subsequent visits to the United States, having been exposed to still more baskets in different shapes and styles, I have grown to appreciate the various possibilities. I now have many American friends and have had the opportunity to teach many students here and abroad.

My special thanks go to Ann Harrow, for encouraging more trips to the United States after we met in 1994 at Wolf Trap Farm Park in Virginia and supporting my every step. Ann's mother, Helen, graciously invited me to her home in Massachusetts.

I'm grateful to Jim Widess for the bravery with which he undertook this book project and for all the work he put in seeing it through. To my translator, Judy Canyock, for translating my Russian into English for this book. To Flo Hoppe, who visited the mosquito-infested Russian forest to see how to harvest birch bark and has written instructions for the projects. To Judy and Lloyd Kramer, who helped me so much with taking photographs of my baskets for slide shows. To Donna Carlson and Lorraine Weiskamp, who visited me in Russia and helped me so much in the United States.

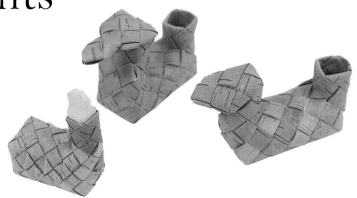

Woven containers, Vladimir Yarish.

In Russia, I want to thank the staff of the Novgorod State Museum of History, Architecture, and Fine Arts, and especially Nikolay Grenyov, Tatiana Matekhina, Natalia Parshina, Ludmila Parshina, Galina Kozina, Nadezda Goreeva, and Evgeniy Gordyushenkov for helping me in my investigation of the birch-bark artifacts at the museum. My colleagues at the Novgorod City Cultural Palace, especially Lubov Shestakova, Natalia Krasnova, and Natalia Kokorina. My students at the basketry guild in Velikiy Novgorod. I also thank my students Alexander Kudriashov, Andrey Terentiev, and Alexander Belov for helping me take photos of harvesting birch bark in the forest.

I'm grateful to the many, many friends in America and Russia who helped me with my work at home and abroad.

And most of all, I thank my wife Tatiana and my son George, who support me in all my projects.

—Vladimir Yarish

When Vladimir lured me into the mosquito-ridden Russian forest several years ago to learn how to harvest birch bark, I had no idea that I would eventually be writing the instructions for his book on birch-bark basketry. This has been an eye-opening journey into the history and intricacies of Russian birch-bark basketry that I will never forget. Vladimir has been a delight to work with, and I will miss the almost daily interactions that we've had via e-mail. I look forward to working with him again—though not necessarily in the Russian forest! Thanks to Jim for getting this project on track and for the excellent photography. Thanks, too, to Ann Harrow for making all the arrangements to bring Vladimir to our country so that he could share his considerable skills. And a special thanks to my husband Don, who shared the Russian forest and Russian bath experiences with me.

—Flo Hoppe

I've been fascinated with birch bark ever since my brother, Paul, sent me a letter written on birch bark from Camp Chippewa in Minnesota many years ago. Thank you to Ann Harrow for bringing Vladimir to the United States so that he could share his incredible skills, techniques, and knowledge with us. Deep appreciation to my wife Sher and my son Andy for giving up family time so that I could work on this project. And much gratitude to the folks at The Caning Shop—Shelly, Jenny, Tami, Lerryn, and Andre—for giving me the time and space to photograph the work in this book. I also would like to acknowledge and thank our editor at Sterling Publishing, Jeanette Green, as well as Laurel Ornitz, who copyedited the manuscript, and *tabula rasa* graphic design, the book designers.

—Jim Widess